THE GLOBAL IMPACT OF THE GREAT DEPRESSION

Dietmar Rothermund broadens the conventional focus of analysis of the Great Depression to include its impact on the countries of Africa, Asia and Latin America. The book:

- gives the economic background to the depression;
- examines the causes of the depression, from the international gold standard to agricultural over-production in the US;
- describes the effects on different countries from America to India, Africa and Far East Asia;
- pays particular attention to the impact on the peasantry in developing countries;
- considers the political consequences, such as fascism in Europe;
- assesses the aftermath and the re-alignment of America, Europe and its colonies;
- explains key areas, such as Keynesian theory, in accessible terms.

Dietmar Rothermund is Professor of South Asian History at the University of Heidelberg. He is the author of several books including *An Economic History of India* (1988) and, with Hermann Kulke, *A History of India* (1990).

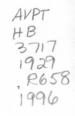

THE GLOBAL IMPACT OF THE GREAT DEPRESSION

1929–1939

Dietmar Rothermund

London and New York

First published 1996 by Routledge
11 New Fetter Lane, London EC4P 4EE
Simultaneously published in the USA and Canada by
Routledge
29 West 35th Street, New York, NY 10001

Routledge is an International Thomson Publishing company

©1996 Dietmar Rothermund

Typeset in Palatino by Routledge
Printed and bound in Great Britain by
TJ Press (Padstow) Ltd, Padstow, Cornwall

British Library Cataloguing in Publication Data
A catalogue record for this book is available from the British Library

Library of Congress Cataloguing in Publication Data
Rothermund, Dietmar.
The Global impact of the Great Depression, 1929–1939/Dietmar
Rothermund.
p. cm.
Includes bibliographical references and index.
1. Depressions–1929–Developing countries. 2. Developing
countries–Economic conditions. 3. Economic history–1918–1945.
I. Title
HB3717 1929.R658 1996
338.5′42–dc20   95–25780
CIP

ISBN 0–415–11818–2 (hbk)
ISBN 0–415–11819–0 (pbk)

CONTENTS

CONTENTS

CONTENTS

PREFACE

Global history is getting a great deal of attention at present. In contrast with the old concepts of universal history and world history which devote a great deal of attention to the origin of civilisations and the transmission of cultural traditions, this new concept encompasses the history of human interaction which at present manifests itself in a highly complex world system. But global history is not limited to the most recent past. It attempts to integrate all fields of historical and anthropological research which contribute to an understanding of the dynamics of human interaction. It transcends national history but it does not neglect the nation state as a unit of international cooperation and conflict.

The Great Depression was an alarming phenomenon of the breakdown of cooperation among nation states which then led to global conflict. While most studies have concentrated on the advanced industrial countries of the world which produced the depression and were also considered to be its major victims, its global impact has hardly attracted any attention. Global historiography is still in its infancy, but this little book may serve as a contribution to this new venture.

The awareness of the global impact of the Great Depression dawned upon me when I was working on the history of agrarian relations in India. I was amazed at the problems faced by the Indian peasantry in the 1930s and found out that there were parallels elsewhere. Turning to Charles Kindleberger's masterly survey *The World in Depression* I found hardly a trace of these problems in his account. In 1978 I sent the first paper which I had produced on 'India in the Great Depression' to him. He kindly replied that he knew next to nothing about Asia and encouraged me to go ahead with my work. I was puzzled by the general neglect

of this subject in the relevant literature and made some of my
German colleagues 'depression minded'; they then designed some
research projects and guided PhD students in this direction. We
also published a volume of (German) essays in 1982 on the
periphery (Africa, Asia, Latin America) in the Great Depression.

In the meantime I did further research and completed a
monograph on 'India in the Great Depression, 1929–1939' which
was published in 1992. While doing this I also collected more
information on other countries as I did not want to present India as
an isolated case. I devoted several lecture courses at Heidelberg
University to this subject which finally added up to a small
German textbook, published in 1993. This I showed to my
publisher in London and by good fortune the text was sent to
Professor Sidney Pollard for evaluation. I benefited from his
constructive criticism and have tried to follow his suggestions in
rewriting the text for the English edition. I must, of course, add the
usual disclaimer: any errors or heretical views still to be found in
the text should be attributed to me alone.

Writing such a 'global' text is no easy task. My main aim was to
put those countries on the map which have so far been neglected
with regard to the study of the impact of the Great Depression. But
as the depression originated in the industrial countries of the West,
I had to take those countries into account, too. This I tried to do as
briefly as possible so as not to duplicate Charles Kindleberger's
work. I start with an introduction entitled 'Economics and the
Depression' in which I also refer to the blind spot in economic
thought which has so far precluded the kind of study which I am
presenting here. Then follows a chapter on the tragedy of the
international gold standard which begins with the 'Golden Age' of
the time before the First World War and then describes the
consequences of the return to the gold standard after the war.
The subsequent chapter concerns the dilemma of war debts and
reparations which further complicated international financial
relations. The fourth chapter is devoted to agricultural production,
because the overproduction of wheat greatly strained the international credit system and finally contributed to its breakdown. The
prices of other crops were then affected by this fall in prices
although the relations of supply and demand for them were stable
and some of them did not even enter the international market.
Since most of the second part of the book deals with the fate of the
peasantry in the countries belonging to the periphery of the world

economy, this chapter on agrarian production is of crucial importance.

With the chapter on the United States of America I begin the survey of the major countries of the world. I must warn the reader that this 'global' survey inevitably has many gaps. I present case studies and do not provide an encyclopaedic coverage of all countries. After concluding that survey I pay attention to the political consequences of the depression and to the fateful sequence war–depression–war which marred about one third of the twentieth century and left a deep impression on global history.

In a text like this which presents a great deal of information and research in a nutshell almost every sentence would require a footnote. Since this would be too cumbersome I have omitted such references and added bibliographical notes at the end of the book. Their sequence parallels the text. The sub-headings which have been repeated in the notes enable the reader to locate the references. There is no separate bibliography, but the names of authors are listed in the index.

In concluding this preface I want to record my thanks to various institutions which supported my research work in recent years – though not necessarily the specific work on this textbook. I would specifically mention the South Asia Institute of Heidelberg University, the German Research Council and the Volkswagen Foundation, the Archive of the Bank of England, the India Office Library, London, and the National Archives of India, New Delhi. Last but not least I thank the Routledge team without whose help and advice this book would not have been published.

Dietmar Rothermund
Heidelberg, June 1995

1

INTRODUCTION
Economics and the depression

THE DEPRESSION AS A CHALLENGE TO
ECONOMIC DOCTRINE

The Great Depression continues to be a challenge to economic
doctrine which is based on the assumption of an equilibrium
produced by the uninhibited working of market forces. There may
be periodical deviations from such an equilibrium, but it will
always be restored after a period of time. The projection of
business cycles fits into such a general theory of an economic
equilibrium as it postulates a regular sequence of upswings and
downturns. Many attempts have been made to fit the Great
Depression into such a regular pattern, but its impact was so
sharp and unprecedented that it cannot be explained in this way. It
seems that it was a unique event and such events can only be
explained historically as they defy the laws of economics. Thus
economists should have returned to 'business as usual', relegating
the depression to the dustbin of history. But they continue to be
fascinated by it and it has given rise to new departures in the field
of economic theory.

First of all the depression has generated an abiding interest in
theories concerning money and credit which had earlier played
only a marginal role in economic thought. Economists used to
concentrate on the exchange of goods, the laws of supply and
demand, etc. In this sphere money was presumed to play a neutral
role, it was a mere medium of exchange which could not affect the
'real economy' in a substantial way. But the depression upset many
assumptions concerning the working of market forces in the 'real
economy'. Credit was suddenly contracted, prices fell to such an
extent that the law of supply and demand seemed to be irrelevant,

1

the international exchange of goods dwindled and many nations returned to the policy prescriptions of the mercantilists who had interpreted trade as a zero sum game in which gains in one place must invariably lead to losses elsewhere. The liberal theory of free trade as an engine of universal growth seemed to be discredited. The beneficial operations of the 'invisible hand' of market forces had obviously been upset by an arbitrary intervention of other forces. The credit system and monetary forces were obviously at fault, but it was not easy to arrive at new theories which would attribute an independent role to such forces, which had been regarded as dependent variables of economic activity.

Monetarism took a long time to come into its own. It attributes a dominant role to the steadiness of money supply in the field of economic growth and deprecates the knee jerk reactions of monetary authorities which may precipitate a downturn by restricting money supply, and unnecessarily fuel an upswing by a policy of easy money. The monetarists explained the causes of the Great Depression by fixing the blame for such knee jerk reactions on the Federal Reserve Board of the United States. This was certainly an important element among the causes of the depression. However, the focus on the Federal Reserve Board was somewhat myopic. In recent years the problems of the international gold standard have attracted attention and their analysis has given more depth and substance to the monetarist explanation of the depression. This will be discussed in detail in the next chapter.

In terms of economic theory monetarism is an attempt at rescuing the old doctrine of economic equilibrium by making money supply the independent variable which determines the working of the 'real economy'. But whereas in the 'real economy' the forces of the market are supposed to generate equilibrium by themselves, in the monetary sphere equilibrium has to be induced by the careful working of the monetary authorities. While it owed a great deal to the test case of the Great Depression, monetarism would have been of no use in prescribing a cure for a world in depression, because it stresses the long term steadiness of money supply rather than short term interventions. It could only provide recommendations for a recovery in the long run. In this way it has triumphed in recent years after the lessons which J.M. Keynes derived from the depression have been largely discredited. But later generations of economists have been unfair to this great heretic who derived a theory of economic disequilibrium from his

2

experience of the Great Depression. His critics took issue with his time bound policy prescriptions, his later admirers did even more harm to him by trying to reinterpret his theory so as to fit it into the mainstream of the doctrine of economic equilibrium. Since his work has left a deep imprint on the interpretation of the Great Depression a brief sketch of the development of his theory will be provided here. This sketch also serves as a survey of the terminology which the reader will encounter in subsequent chapters.

KEYNES AND THE THEORY OF ECONOMIC DISEQUILIBRIUM

Keynes was mainly interested in monetary theory and he had worked in this field long before he encountered the Great Depression. He noticed the deep gap between the theory of the exchange of goods and monetary theory and made a lasting contribution to economics by introducing central issues discussed in the first field to the discourse of monetary economics. Monetary theory had so far concentrated on the quantity of money and the velocity of its circulation and its impact on prices. Elasticities of supply and demand which were discussed with regard to the exchange of goods were not even mentioned in monetary theory as they were considered to be irrelevant in this sphere. Pre-Keynesian monetary theory was also wedded to a rather mechanical doctrine of equilibrium and to the basic assumption of the neutrality of money as a medium of exchange. The great insight of Keynes, that money links the present with the future and is therefore linked to all elements of uncertainty which beset predictions of the future course of events, was of no concern to earlier monetary theorists.

In his early works on monetary theory Keynes did not question neoclassical doctrine and the quantity theory of money. But he was already grappling with the phenomenon of 'liquidity preference', i.e. the propensity to hold on to money rather than to invest it or to spend it on goods and services. He had come across this phenomenon in his work on *Indian Currency and Finance* (1913) where he referred to liquidity preference as a strong passion of the Indian people which was detrimental to the creation of real wealth. But this work was dedicated to the advocacy of a gold exchange standard for India, i.e. a standard based on gold but without the circulation of gold coins. The reference to Indian 'liquidity preference' was an ancillary argument in this context; it was not yet a major issue for Keynes.

In his work *A Treatise on Money* he discussed liquidity preference in detail, but he was not quite satisfied with his conclusions and moved towards a closer integration of monetary theory with other fields of economic theory. The experience of the depression influenced the development of his thought at that time. In 1932 he suddenly changed the title of his lecture course at Cambridge from 'A Pure Theory of Money' to 'A Theory of Money and Production'. In this context liquidity preference acquired a new meaning: it referred to the speculative demand for money as an element of instability of financial markets due to the uncertain character of expectations about the future level of the interest rate. Such speculative demand could upset the economy and called for active intervention of the monetary authorities. Keynes highlighted the potential of disruptive activities as well as the necessity of countervailing measures. In his *General Theory of Employment, Interest and Money* he presented his conclusions in a provocative manner. He deliberately emphasised those points which had been neglected by the prevailing economic doctrine. The theory of the exchange of goods had been dominated by supply-side economics, whereas he stressed the crucial importance of demand. In monetary theory, which was characterised by demand-side economics, he pointed to speculative liquidity preference which determined the supply of funds available for investment and expenditure on goods and services. In discussing liquidity preference in this way he introduced the discourse concerning the elasticities of supply and demand into monetary theory.

Neoclassical theory on the exchange of goods had been based on the assumption that supply would always create a corresponding demand because there would always be a clearing of the market. Inelasticies of supply and demand were marginal phenomena: an oversupply of goods may not be cleared even at a very low price and some goods could not be provided even at a much higher price. The labour market was seen as an analogy to the market for goods. All labour offered in the market would find employment, though perhaps at a low wage; involuntary unemployment was therefore inconceivable. Inelasticities of supply and demand in the labour market or in the money market were not taken into consideration. Just as labour would find employment, income had either to be saved, and thus available for investment, or it would be spent on goods and services. Hoarding of money was, of course, known to economists but they thought of it as a kind of marginal friction just as there may be frictions in the labour market when labour set free in one place would take time to shift to new employment elsewhere.

In keeping with these assumptions the universal prescription of employers under the impact of the depression was a lowering of wages, which had become sticky. Actually, during the depression nominal wages proved to be very sticky indeed, and real wages increased because prices fell. Thus the complaint of the employers seemed to have some substance. Keynes held against this that the lowering of wages would only reduce the demand for goods and services and the money saved by employers after a reduction of wages would not necessarily be available for investment due to their liquidity preference which was bound to be particularly strong in a depression. According to these basic assumptions the interest rate which had so far been considered to be the price of money determined by the demand for it was to Keynes rather the premium to be paid to the holder of money so as to entice him to give up his liquidity preference.

In the crucial Chapter 19 of his *General Theory* Keynes could thus attack the clamour for the reduction of wages by pointing out that such a reduction without a change in money supply would at best have the same effect on the interest rate as an increase in money supply without a reduction of wages. The first course would be much more difficult to follow than the latter. To those who would argue that an increase in money supply would fuel inflation, Keynes answered that this fear was unfounded as long as there was no full employment. He highlighted the asymmetry of deflation and inflation: deflation depressed effective demand below the level of full employment and reduced both prices and employment whereas inflation would push up prices only once the level of full employment had been reached. He conceded that prices might rise slightly even before full employment had been achieved.

This 'general theory' was designed so as to apply to a closed national economy. It could be argued that Keynes used this as an expository device and refrained from dealing with the international context because this would have complicated his work. But there was more to it than this: Keynes was actually facing a national economy in Great Britain which could be treated as a kind

5

of closed economy after the gold standard had been abandoned in 1931 and the management of the British economy was no longer geared to maintaining London as a centre of world finance. In fact, Keynes was wise in restricting the exposition of his theory to a closed national economy. If he had commented on the international context at that time, he would have shown his hand as a convinced neo-mercantilist. This would have attracted even more criticism than that which he provoked with his *General Theory* anyhow. His respect for the mercantilists did show up in a passage of his *General Theory* where he argued that even in a closed national economy the interest rate may not reach a sufficiently low level to encourage investment and production. Intervention may be required to reach such a level. The mercantilists, so he said, had devoted much attention to full employment and the interest rate whereas the classical economists of a later age had neglected this field.

In the days of the Great Depression the actual influence of Keynes on economic policy was restricted to his recommendations concerning money supply whereas his fiscal prescriptions, which he considered more important (deficit spending, etc.), were not taken up. The prevailing orthodoxy with regard to a balanced budget was only one reason for this disregard of fiscal measures. There was also the practical reason that governments at that time did not have sufficient statistical information to monitor fiscal policy. Parallel to the Keynesian revolution there was a quiet and imperceptible revolution in statistics and national accounting which enabled economists and governments at a later stage to know what they were doing when following a Keynesian policy. Keynes himself did not yet benefit from this quiet revolution and therefore his later critics could complain that his theory was mostly based on qualitative statements and not on econometric research. Nevertheless his contribution will always be remembered as he answered the challenge of the Great Depression by means of a provocative theory.

NEO-MERCANTILISM OR 'BEGGAR-THY-NEIGHBOUR'

The problem of international economic relations which Keynes did not discuss in the *General Theory* was boldly addressed by his young contemporary Joan Robinson, who stated that under the impact of the depression most nations had adopted the principle of 'beggar-thy-neighbour'. They had adopted a policy of protectionism, competitive devaluation and similar devices all aimed at restoring their own benefits from trade at the cost of others. She referred to the remarks which Keynes had made on mercantilism and argued that in times of worldwide unemployment a country may very well increase its employment and total output by increasing its trade balance at the expense of its competitors.

The most obvious means of correcting a negative trade balance is the devaluation of the national currency as this makes exports cheaper and imports more expensive and is thus immediately much more effective than a combination of protective tariffs with export subsidies. The problem with a devaluation is, of course, that there may not be a great deal of elasticity of demand for a country's exports, i.e. their availability at a cheaper price would not attract more buyers, and on the other hand the demand for imports may not decline if it concerns essential supplies such as investment goods and petroleum. In the latter case the country may actually import an inflation as the higher prices of imports push up domestic prices in general. Another problem faced by a country after devalution is how to restrain the absorption capacity of the domestic economy. If this capacity keeps pace with the increase of exportable output not much of it may be left. This absorption capacity tends to adjust to the new conditions and therefore the first devaluation is often followed by another one.

Under the impact of the depression most devaluations were precipitated by an acute balance of payments crisis which left the respective government no other choice. But there were also voluntary and rather deliberate ones, the most prominent of them being the devaluation of the US dollar in 1933, which was not caused by any external problems but was rather aimed at importing a certain dose of inflation so as to reflate the domestic economy. The imported inflation which usually comes as an unwanted consequence of a devaluation was deliberately induced in this way by President Roosevelt and his advisers.

Devaluations in the proper sense of the term are always 'pegged' ones, i.e. the respective government renounces the prevalent exchange rate and proclaims a new rate defined in terms of gold or a prominent foreign currency. 'Pegging' has the disadvantage that it is very difficult to know whether the new rate is either too high or too low. The more elegant way of adjusting the currency is to renounce the relation of the currency to gold or any other currency, just letting it 'float' until it finds its new value in the international market. Such 'floating' is often announced with the declared intention to 'peg' the currency at a later stage when it has found its proper level. But often 'floating' proves to be so attractive that 'pegging' is postponed – the 'floating pound' is a case in point, about which more will be said in subsequent chapters. The problem with 'floating' is that it makes transactions in the respective currency unpredictable and forces merchants to refer to a foreign currency when settling their bills. It is therefore more likely that a prominent currency is allowed to 'float' whereas others are bound to be 'pegged'.

The period of the Great Depression offers many examples of more or less successful devaluations. But these experiences have not given rise to a 'general theory' and there is as yet no agreement on how monetary policy should be conducted at the international level. Joan Robinson drew attention to the problem by formulating her 'beggar-thy-neighbour' thesis, but she did not follow it up with more detailed work. The main problem is, of course, the reaction of the neighbours to this kind of policy. They can be expected to retaliate, thus starting a vicious circle which leads to a further contraction of trade and an increase of unemployment. Hit by the depression most countries concerned did not have much time to consider the consequences of their actions. Many countries accompanied the devaluation with a suspension of debt service to their foreign creditors. These creditors in turn retaliated by providing no further credit thus contributing to the worldwide credit contraction which deepened and lengthened the depression so that it really deserved to be called 'great'.

The countries of the depressed world can be divided roughly into three categories: those who moved in sympathy with the British pound, those who looked to the US dollar, and those who tried to maintain their link with the gold standard. The first category, which included Portugal and the Scandinavian countries as well as the British colonies, followed the 'floating pound'. Sweden did so by passing a specific law within a week of the British decision to abandon the gold standard. The Norwegian government could do so by decree as there was already a law on the statute book enabling it to take this decision should the need arise. The British colonial currencies remained linked to the pound and floated with it. South Africa, which was autonomous, could have stuck to the gold standard because as a gold producing country it had sufficient reserves, but it also devalued its currency in 1932, because so much had been talked about an impending devaluation that a great deal of capital had left the country. Finally the government had to take action: an exemplary case of a self-fulfilling prophecy. Australia was another special case, which will be discussed in detail later on.

The second category consisted mostly of the Latin American countries. Their devaluations were caused by acute difficulties as far as their balance of payments were concerned. Chile performed the most spectacular feat in this region. It had returned to the gold standard in 1926 but abandoned it in July 1931 even before Great Britain took that step. The currency was then allowed to float and depreciated by 40 per cent in relation to gold. Subsequently a socialist government, which was only in power for about three month, printed bank notes, thus increasing money supply in order to fight unemployment. The socialist government was eliminated by a military coup, but the inflationary policy was also pursued by the new rulers. This caused an internal depreciation of the currency which then led to a further devaluation. In this case the inflation was not an imported but a home-grown one. Other Latin American countries experienced similar developments, but none of them matched Chile in this.

The third category, which consisted of those countries which decided to stick to the gold standard, had a hard time in doing so while their neighbours devalued their currencies or permitted them to float. They had to adopt the most brutal mercantilist policies such as imposing an embargo on the export of gold as well as foreign exchange controls and conducting their foreign trade in terms of barter agreements. Most of them had to abandon the gold standard sooner or later. Japan provided a particularly striking case in point which will be discussed in detail later on. It had joined the gold standard as late as 1930, then clung to it with a vengeance and finally opted for a most radical devaluation in 1932.

Whereas the 'beggar-thy-neighbour' phenomenon and the process of competitive devaluation did at least attract the attention of economists, although they did not come up with a 'general theory' in this field, they were almost totally blind as far as the fate of the peasantry at the periphery of the world economy was concerned. This is not simply due to practical ignorance but to a theoretical bias which will be discussed in the following section.

9

A BLIND SPOT: THE FATE OF THE PERIPHERY

As has been shown above the great economic debate concerning the causes and cures of the depression centred on the problem of industrial unemployment. The second focus of the debate was on international debt service and balance of payments problems. If a country had no industrial unemployment in the 1930s and if it did not even have a balance of payments problem, it was obviously very lucky and had escaped the impact of the depression. India is a case in point: its industrial labour force, which was still very small in those days, faced no unemployment for reasons which will be explained in the relevant chapter. India's balance of payments was positive throughout the years of the depression because of the large outflow of 'distress gold' released by indebted peasants. The steep fall of agrarian prices in India was, of course, taken note of by the economists, but this was of no concern to them, because a sectoral fall in prices must necessarily benefit other sectors of the economy. Indeed, real wages of industrial workers increased during the depression years in India because food was cheap. They never had such a good time before or after the depression. For all these reasons even Indian economists who have been properly trained along the lines of accepted economic wisdom would hold the view that India had escaped the impact of the depression.

This blind spot, which is so firmly grounded in economic doctrine, has prevented the study of the impact of the depression on the periphery of the world economy for a long time. At the most some attention has been paid to the supposedly positive effect which the depression had on the industries located in peripheral countries which could benefit from import substitution. The peripheral peasantry which bore the brunt of the impact of the depression has remained in the dark, its fate has not entered economic consciousness.

In addition to the factors which have already been mentioned with regard to the 'blind spot', there is another one which comes up when the fate of the peasantry is discussed. It is the belief in subsistence agriculture which supposedly absorbs those who cannot make a living in a depressed economy. Of course, if a peasant can grow his own food and can almost totally withdraw from the market economy the depression would not affect him. But by the 1930s subsistence agriculture was already a myth as far as most of the peasants were concerned. Money lenders, traders and

10

tax collectors had caught up with the peasants almost everywhere. Colonial governments knew very well about the pressure they exerted on the peasantry to produce for the market in order to pay taxes. Produce grown for export then yielded another revenue income derived from export taxes. Hit by the depression the governments concerned were in no mood to reduce taxes, thus there was no escape for the peasant into the safe realm of subsistence agriculture.

The real crux was the self-perpetuating peasant indebtedness caused by the need to borrow money from the money lender when the tax collector came. Many governments actually encouraged this vicious circle as it forced peasants to produce for the market, because if they did not do so, revenue income was bound to decline. In the deflationary regimes which caused the depression, debts appreciated while prices fell. On top of this the money lenders were keen to recover their capital as they were no longer sure about their debtors' future capacity to service their debts. The American economist, Irving Fisher, proposed a 'debt–deflation theory' of the depression in 1932 which reflected his immediate experience at that time. This theory was geared to an industrial economy and did not refer to indebted peasants, but it may also throw some light on their problems. Fisher argued that debt-financed innovations may give rise to a boom while in a subsequent recession accompanied by deflation the economy may be caught in a debt trap and remain depressed unless it is reflated by the authorities concerned. The peasants at the periphery had certainly not experienced a boom caused by innovations, but agricultural prices were rather high in the 1920s and agricultural credit was freely available. When the recession began, due to the overproduction of certain types of produce, this affected agricultural prices in general. The deflationary policy was for the most part exogenous, i.e. transmitted from abroad and enforced by authorities acting under the compulsion of international creditors. The peasants then saw what a debt–deflation trap looks like and only in some rare instances were they promptly relieved by reflation. In most countries they remained in the trap for several years.

Peasant unrest was widespread in the countries of the periphery in the 1930s. But in most cases it remained localised and did not attract international attention. Several instances will be reported in subsequent chapters. A full survey would fill volumes and require

11

much detailed research. The story was almost always the same: the repressive machinery of the state was quick to crush peasant resistance, and as peasants were scarcely armed and poorly organised the police or the army could vanquish them very quickly. Only in extremely rare cases were national movements or parties able to turn peasant unrest into a political asset.

Globally the industrial centres of the world managed to shift the burden of the depression to the countries of the periphery and within those countries the urban areas prospered at the cost of the rural ones. The principle of 'beggar-thy-neighbour' thus had a much more universal application than that which Joan Robinson had in mind when she coined the term.

THE WEB OF CREDIT

In this final section of the introductory chapter an attempt will be made to link the many subsequent case studies of the impact of the depression to a main theme: the spread and recoil of the web of credit which connected the financial centres of the world with rural money lenders and indebted peasants at the periphery of the world economy. Credit – like money – links the present with the future, but it also links it with the past in terms of debts accumulated in earlier years. Credit always involves trust and risk, but there are several factors which may limit the dependence on trust and the hazards of risk, e.g. a uniform standard of value, well defined property rights, cheap and easy enforcement of contracts and free access to information concerning the debtor's past and present standing and his future prospects. Where all these factors can be taken for granted, credit transactions can be anonymous and highly specific. Debt service will be moderate as transaction costs are low. Creditors will make a profit even if their charges are low, because of the volume and frequency of transactions.

The other end of the scale would be characterised by the absence or deficiency of most of the factors mentioned above. Even if credit transactions are not completely suspended under such adverse conditions, they are at least restricted, personalised and costly. Close supervision of credit will have to compensate for such deficiencies. Because such supervision is costly, debt service will be burdensome. Creditors will have to adopt stratagems which increase their personal control over the debtors. Such stratagems would include the fixing of a high nominal interest rate so that the debt can never be redeemed, while actually charging a flexible effective interest rate as the debtors must be kept alive in order to service their debt. Another stratagem is that of interlinking the granting of credit in several spheres. Thus creditors may market their clients' produce and pay their rent or land revenue demand whenever it is due. Such interlinking is a potent instrument of personal control. Whatever debtors do, they remain in the clutches of their creditors. In fact, debtors may even have to till their creditors' land, carry their burdens and send the women of the family to work in the creditors' household.

The two ends of the scale mentioned here seem to represent different worlds of credit transactions. In fact, if one looks at the high differentials of interest rates one may come to the conclusion that credit markets are split and entirely unrelated to each other. But actually the markets are not split, they are connected by re-financing arrangements all down the line. For instance, bank credit may be provided for forward trading based on the security of stores of grain in the possession of wholesale merchants and such merchants may re-finance local money lenders and grain dealers. In this way the web of credit connects the financial centres of the world with the humble transactions at the periphery. Differences in interest rates would reflect the respective cost of supervision. The uniform standard of value is, of course, the most crucial factor which supports the web of credit and this is why creditors in the interwar period favoured the restoration of the international gold standard. If this required a deflationary monetary policy, it did not hurt creditors because it appreciated debts while inflation would have diminished them. Industrial workers, as long as they were employed, were actually in the same position as creditors: deflation would increase their real wages. The solidarity of the working class was strained in this way. The unemployed could not count on the support of the employed as their interests were opposed to each other's.

As will be explained in the next chapter, the automatism of the international gold standard was supposed to keep inflation and deflation, as well as the expansion of credit, within reasonable bounds. But in the postwar world, which was beset by conflicts of national interests, the return to an international standard of value proved to be a tragic illusion. Once this project had failed, the web of credit did not just collapse, it recoiled. This was bad enough for the industrial countries of the West, but it was particularly damaging for the agricultural countries at the periphery whose credit systems were characterised by the deficiencies mentioned earlier. The fall in agricultural prices which will be discussed in a subsequent chapter was precipitated by the contraction of credit in the core regions of the world economy. It left indebted peasants with greatly reduced incomes and thus their debts became unbearable. The local creditors responded to this not only by stopping further credit, but by trying hard to recover their capital. Forward trading was abandoned and price fluctuations reappeared which had prevailed in the days before the railway and the telegraph had penetrated the respective countries. The structure of agrarian markets was shattered by this recoil of the web of credit and it took a long time to mend it again.

In the meantime a stream of 'distress gold' left many countries of the periphery and flowed to the core countries, helping them to reflate their economies. Money lenders snatched the ornaments of indebted peasants, who parted with them because they would otherwise have been forced to sell their land. Keynes had once said that gold in the pockets of the people would not be available to the government in an emergency, but this flow of gold from the periphery to the core showed that under conditions of agrarian distress this dictum was not true.

But why did the web of credit recoil? Why was the international credit system not resilient enough to cope with the crisis of 1930? At the root of the problem seems to be the inherent contradiction between the two functions of central banking. A central bank should first and foremost act as a lender of last resort, but charged with this responsibility it will also aim at maintaining price stability in the respective country. Walter Bagehot had once formulated a good piece of advice for those who have to act as lenders of last resort: lend freely at high interest rates. But high interest rates would upset price stability and therefore central banks would rather follow a long term policy of supporting price stability. In fact, central banks which have been able to follow such a policy even under adverse conditions have generally been praised for it. The case study of Sweden in Chapter 6 shows this very clearly.

The US Federal Reserve Board (FED), about which more will be said in the next chapter, was actually established only for the purpose of serving as a lender of last resort, but faced with the task

14

of fighting the inflation caused by the First World War it soon turned to the second task mentioned above and saw to it that prices remained stable. In order to do this it actually suspended the automatism of the international gold standard and sterilised gold flowing into America which would have boosted inflation. When the American economy had to be reflated subsequently the FED did not release gold but created its own credit. Benjamin Strong, the Governor of the Federal Reserve Bank of New York, whose position will be described in the next chapter, explained this very clearly to the US House of Representatives in 1926. He said that in the old days bank deposits and the price level varied directly with the stock of gold, but in recent years Reserve Bank credit had become the equivalent of gold. But Strong did not think that this would undermine the international gold standard. On the contrary, he worked very hard in those years to get the European nations back on the gold standard. His two major operations in 1924 and 1927 to ease credit in the United States were aimed less at fighting minor recessions at home than at relieving deflation abroad and thus helping the countries who were rejoining the gold standard. In this way he atoned for having sterilised gold earlier, but at the same time he provided liquidity at home which gave rise to a wave of stock market speculation. He was obviously caught on the horns of a dilemma. After having suspended the automatism of the gold standard he provided Federal Reserve credit – 'the equivalent of gold' as he had rightly called it. But he could not control inflation at home and fight deflation abroad in this way. The basic contradiction of maintaining an international gold standard and a powerful central bank devoted to internal price stability emerged in this way. Strong was obviously confident that he could square the circle.

The crux of the matter was that the creation of Federal Reserve credit could not be geared to the needs of international trade and the maintenance of the web of credit abroad, it had to be aimed at maintaining price stability at home. When the crisis approached the FED was so much concerned with stability that it was no longer able to act as a proper lender of last resort, i.e. lending freely at high interest rates. The basic contradiction of American central banking could not be resolved. The only solution would have been to adhere to the gold standard and permit the free flow of gold, or to abandon it rather than trying to enable as many nations as possible to return to it while sterilising gold at home.

Once the gold standard was abandoned by the majority of nations they turned to the policies of the 'beggar-thy-neighbour' type described earlier. The problem with many countries at the periphery was that they could not even do that as they were colonies which had no control over their monetary and economic policies. The colonial rulers had only their own interests in mind. As the case of India will show, the British profited from keeping the economy of this large colony deflated and depressed as this led to the further flow of 'distress gold'. Reflating colonial economies was a task which none of the colonial powers was willing to shoulder. Moreover, while earlier the access to raw materials and produce was the main reason for acquiring and maintaining colonies, the depression had reduced the prices of all primary commodities to such an extent that colonialism was no longer required for that purpose. Only the national debts of such colonies accumulated in the past made it necessary to keep these debtors under control. To that extent the web of credit was still in place while it had recoiled in every other respect.

The many case studies of countries on the periphery which form the major part of this book illustrate this basic pattern of indebtedness and continuous depression. We have stated earlier that credit links the present with the future as well as with the past. In this situation the link with the past predominated while the future looked dim. The case studies also show how a variety of contingent factors affected the fate of each country. The type of commodities produced, the pattern of taxation, the development of financial, legal and political institutions, would all make a difference with regard to the severity and the duration of the impact of the depression.

The pattern of taxation was of special significance. The major items of revenue income of colonial governments were export and import duties, poll taxes and land revenue. The collection of duties in the ports was most convenient as it yielded a good income with a minimum of administrative expenditure. But under the impact of the depression, duties dwindled and the authorities were forced to fall back on other types of taxation, e.g. poll taxes. Such taxes were most burdensome for the poor as they were assessed per head (or hut) regardless of the income of the taxpayer. Land revenue, which was practically unknown in Africa but was of major importance in Asia, was assessed in terms of the area of land cultivated. This implied that the revenue authorities had to maintain land records, which helped to define property rights although such records were no substitute for a proper record of land titles. The revenue authorities were not interested in the proprietor as such as long as somebody paid the revenue. If nobody paid the revenue they could always confiscate the land and sell it at a public auction.

The type of taxation determined to what extent credit played a role for the taxpayer. If the government depended exclusively on import and export duties, credit would only follow the lines of trade in terms of advances to the cultivators or for the buying and selling of crops to numerous intermediaries. Poll taxes would attract credit if they had a function in the process of interlinking mentioned above. Burma is a case in point, which will be discussed in Chapter 12. The land revenue demand could usually be met only by means of credit provided by petty money lenders. Property rights as defined by the records of the revenue authorities provided enough security to the creditor in this respect. Accordingly colonies such as India, where land revenue was of major importance and the peasantry was indebted, suffered most under the impact of the depression. On the other hand the revenue authorities found it most difficult to revise revenue rates in the years of the depression. Revision had always meant an enhancement of the rates based on the average of prices of the preceding ten years. This worked very well as long as there was a secular trend of rising prices, but the system could not cope with a catastrophic fall in prices. Therefore the land revenue system was practically destroyed by the depression, but this was felt only in the course of time whereas the pressure of existing rates ruined many peasants in the initial years of the depression, particularly if they also had to service previous debts and found their creditors unwilling to provide further credit.

Another important variable was the legal system maintained by the respective colonial power. In many colonies the colonial rulers had introduced their own laws only for their countrymen whereas the 'natives' were left to the devices of their 'customary law'. Of course, the interpretation of 'customary law' was liable to change under colonial rule, but it was for the most part less watertight as far as the protection of creditors was concerned than the British law introduced in India, where even the instrument of the ex parte decree was available to all creditors. This meant that the judge did not have to hear the debtor in court, but could arrive at a judgment by looking at the bond signed by the debtor and presented to him by the creditor. Money lenders often used this not to evict their debtors, but to force them to sign even more extortionate bonds so as to keep them permanently under their control. Where the web of credit was strengthened by such legal instruments it was particularly tight and could strangle the debtors when it recoiled and did not expand again.

A full survey of the impact of the depression would have to spell out in detail the way in which the web of credit recoiled and what kind of legal and economic consequences this had for the respective debtors. For most countries of the periphery this information is not yet available because of the lack of relevant research. The 'blind spot' mentioned earlier is responsible for this lack of research. Accordingly the case studies presented here can only provide outlines of the impact of the depression based on the results of research work published so far. The remarks on the web of credit made in this introductory chapter may help the reader not to lose sight of the wood by looking at so many trees. At the same time these remarks will also make a reader aware of the many gaps in these case studies which will have to be filled by further research.

2

THE TRAGEDY OF THE INTERNATIONAL GOLD STANDARD

In the chaotic times after the First World War, the prewar world appeared to have been paradise and there was a nostalgic feeling that one should return to it as soon as possible. This was particularly true of the international gold standard which had prevailed at that time and which most countries had to abandon during the war. This standard had guaranteed monetary stability and economic growth for several decades, which now looked like a golden age. The advantages of such a standard had already been praised by David Hume and David Ricardo, because it provided an equilibrium by means of a simple mechanism which seemed to work as if governed by a law of nature.

In direct opposition to bullionists and mercantilists Hume and Ricardo recommended the free flow of the precious metals. If they flowed out of a country they would thereby lower the prices and their inflow would increase the prices elsewhere, which would then lead to their flowing back to countries where prices were lower. This process would work best without any interference. Not even a central bank was required, but if it did exist it would work best if it only accentuated the mechanism of the free flow of the precious metals. It would raise the discount rate when the precious metals flowed out of the country, thus lowering prices by enhancing deflation, and it would lower the discount rate whenever precious metals were flowing in, thus providing easy money and increasing prices.

As a matter of fact, the belief in the beneficial qualities of the gold standard was a tragic illusion. This standard did not work automatically at all but depended on the existence of a powerful lender of last resort, an institution which was able to ensure the liquidity and stability of the world market. At the same time the firm belief in the gold standard was necessary in order to maintain the confidence in this lender of last resort. Thus the tragic illusion was a necessary one and it proved to be tragic for this very reason.

The international lender of last resort in the golden age before the First World War was the Bank of England which supported the gold standard and was supported by it. Therefore it was desperate to return to the gold standard after the war, as will be described in the third section of this chapter. After it had achieved this in 1925, the last act of the tragedy began. It ended in the depression. This we can see with the benefit of hindsight, but those who returned to the gold standard in the postwar period saw it differently. Blinded by the tragic illusion, they felt they were restoring the stability of the golden age. They did not know that what they considered to be a great achievement was in fact a terrible mistake. The period between achievement and disaster was particularly dramatic in Japan which returned to the gold standard only in 1930 and had to abandon it by the end of 1931. A few months later the finance minister who was responsible for the return to the gold standard was murdered by men who obviously felt that he had betrayed the interests of the Japanese people – as indeed he had, though with the best of intentions.

THE BANK OF ENGLAND AND THE GOLD STANDARD

The Bank of England was a private bank which belonged to private shareholders. Its governor determined monetary policy, or rather he supposedly supervised the smooth operation of the mechanism which has been described above. The bank could dictate the rules of the game, because it issued the premier currency of the world, the pound sterling, which was unassailable as long Great Britain always had a positive balance of payments. This positive balance was mainly due to 'invisibles' i.e. interest paid on exported capital, charges for financial services and, of course, the tributes from the colonies. The term 'tribute' may sound incongruous in an age of capitalism as it is associated with feudalism, but in the colonial context it reflects quite accurately the imposition of charges by foreign rulers without the consent of the people concerned, e.g. pensions and remittances of expatriate staff, the cost of the metropolitan headquarters such as the India Office in London, debt service on government bonds issued by the colonial rulers for purposes which they determined, etc. Such charges flowed to the City of London as the centre of the largest colonial empire of all times. With all this the City had plenty of funds to invest elsewhere. At the end of the nineteenth century London annually sent a stream of capital amounting to £100 million to countries abroad. In the first decade of the twentieth century this rose to £170 million. America – both North and South – always received the lion's share of this capital export, whereas India received only 10 per cent. The dividend and interest earned on this capital amounted on average to about 10 per cent while normal interest on bank deposits was well below 5 per cent. If we assume that ten times the amount of capital exported annually had not yet been paid back and was yielding interest, this interest would be equivalent to the annual investment abroad. But, of course, a great deal of this investment was for much longer periods and thus capital export was not just self-perpetuating but provided a steadily increasing income to the financial centre of the world.

It has sometimes been argued that British colonies were particularly fortunate, because they had easy access to this enormous capital market. Those who wanted to prove the direct link between imperialism and finance capitalism were eager to emphasise this point. But recent studies of the political economy of British imperialism have shown that this assumption is wrong. The colonies were not the foremost targets of British capital exports. Their exploitation was managed by different means.

In addition to the steady flow of returns on its capital exports abroad, Great Britain had many other resources at its disposal with which it could manage the international gold standard. Before France demonetised silver, London could make use of the buffer function of the bimetallic (gold and silver) French currency, later on British control of the Indian silver currency and the inflow of South African gold were grist to the mill of this financial centre of the world. Bimetallism and the importance of silver will be discussed in the next section of this chapter. At this stage it is sufficient to state that London not only controlled the flow of gold but also that of silver and was thus in an even better position to manage the international gold standard.

Holding a key position as the hub of the world financial centre, the Bank of England could also perform the task of a lender of last resort for the United States of America until the Federal Reserve Board was established in 1913. The United States had an extremely chaotic banking system and its gold reserves were under the control of the US Treasury which did nothing with them but simply stored them. Alexander Hamilton, who was in charge of state finance after the United States attained independence, wanted to establish an American central bank along the lines of the Bank of England, but he was unable to get this done because of the recalcitrance of the various states. The fact that the United States could do without a central bank for such a long time reflected the predominance of local interests in a nation of farmers and manufacturers. International traders and banks providing global financial services were marginal to the American economy.

In striking contrast to the American scene the City of London depended on its income from financial services and was attuned to the working of the world market. Walter Bagehot, the editor of *The Economist*, who had started his career as a banker, remarked in the 1870s that the population of Great Britain would soon consist only of money lenders and their servants. This was a sarcastic remark, but it did reflect the trend of British economic development. Because the interests of international money lenders prevailed, British monetary policy was global rather than dictated by domestic compulsions. This was resented by British industry, but the weight of the City of London was so great that other interests had no chance to go against it. Accordingly the Bank of England played a role which was rather different from that of the American Federal Reserve Board, which was more influenced by domestic compulsions than by considerations of international finance. The board felt that its major duty was the maintenance of domestic price stability. To that extent its policy was monetarist long before monetarism was invented. But opting for a steady money supply in the interest of this stability was, of course, contrary to the principles of the gold standard which were based on letting the flow of gold determine the price level. When gold flowed into the United States after the First World War, this should have meant a strong upward pressure on American prices, but the board counteracted this by sterilising gold, thus practically suspending the gold standard mechanism.

The Federal Reserve Board was by no means intent on ruining the international gold standard in this way: it was, in fact, deeply attached to it while at the same time violating the rules of the game. The tragedy of the gold standard thus reached its climax in the interwar years due to the fateful change of guards when America

22

replaced Great Britain as the major financial power. For the Bank of England international finance was central, for the Federal Reserve Board it was peripheral, but its responses to American domestic issues had immediate consequences in the international field.

The functions of the Bank of England as a kind of world central bank were challenged even before the First World War by two kinds of competitors wanting to play their own game. There were first of all some national central banks which wanted to rival the Bank of England, but did not want to permit the free flow of gold as they usually did not have enough of it. The much more dangerous competitors were the large commercial banks of the City of London which maintained branches all over the world and were mainly interested in short term financial transactions. They were not very much concerned with the measures adopted by the Bank of England in the interest of long term stability. Of course, the directors of those banks were represented on the council of the Bank of England, but this did not necessarily mean that they would subordinate their interests to those of the central bank. Jointly these banks held more funds than the Bank of England, and the governor of the central bank had to possess a great deal of diplomatic skill to deal both with foreign central banks and with his rivals in the city.

Before the war it was the rule that the post of the governor was occupied only for a short time by one of the directors of the member banks. As long as the going was good and the council of the Bank of England was like a bankers' club, this rotation of the post of the governor was no problem. But it was highly significant that when the Bank had to face a totally different financial environment after the First World War, one man emerged as de facto permanent governor and held this post from 1919 to 1944: Montagu Norman. He was also the driving force behind Great Britain's quest for the return to the gold standard. Before describing this crucial event, we shall first turn to an analysis of an important alternative to a monometallic gold standard: bimetallism. A historical flashback to the defeat of bimetallism will throw light on the virtues and vices of the gold standard.

THE DEFEAT OF BIMETALLISM

The exchange relation of gold and silver had stood at 1 to 15 for a very long time. The stability of this relationship depended on the balanced production of both metals. If there was overproduction of one of them, this would upset the delicate balance unless there was so much demand for the overproduced metal elsewhere that the balance would be restored in this way. Since the discovery of American silver there had been an ample supply of this metal, but there had also been a constant flow of silver to Asia where both India and China had silver currencies of huge dimensions. Since they were both large agrarian countries whose governments mostly subsisted on land revenue, the circulation of the currency was very sluggish and more silver coins were required than in an economy dominated by trade where the velocity of circulation is much higher. Thus the absorptive capacity of silver was enormous in China and India. Some time in the eighteenth century the Chinese demand for silver was so high that the exchange relation between gold and silver in that country stood at 1 to 10, which made it highly profitable for Europeans to take silver to China in order to buy gold for it there.

For most countries a bimetallic currency was of great advantage. Silver could be used for normal transactions such as paying taxes or buying daily requirements whereas gold was reserved for large transactions and long distance trade. At a time when the circulation of bank notes or cheques was not yet of major importance and most transactions depended on cash, this circulation of two precious metals was of particular importance. The exchange relation of gold and silver coins was stabilised by a simple mechanism. Whenever one of the metals increased in value due to a shortage of supply or its value decreased because of overproduction, the people would react very quickly. They would melt down the coins whose metal content exceeded their denomination and take the respective metal to the mint in order to get it coined. Of course, this mechanism depended on the free access of the people to the mints and it worked only within certain limits. A sudden oversupply of one of the metals could upset the balance. Thus the arrangement was flexible but it also tended to be volatile. A monometallic gold standard was less flexible but more stable. As most people prefer stability, particularly when long term contracts are involved, a gold standard had much to recommend it. This argument must have been in the mind of Sir Isaac Newton who laid the foundation of the gold standard in 1717 in his capacity as royal mint master. He fixed a low price for silver and a high price for gold and thus practically put an end to the coining of silver. But it was only at the end of the century that Great Britain adopted the gold standard officially after it had prevailed in practice for a long time

The British option for gold was by no means imitated by other countries at that time. France and the United States maintained a bimetallic standard until the 1870s, but they did this in rather different ways. In the United States the bimetallic standard had continued only in a nominal way as no silver coins were in circulation. But silver was officially demonetised only in 1873. France initially bought gold and sold silver, most of which flowed to Asia. But when France finally demonetised silver in 1878, this caused a worldwide fall in the price of that metal. Much of the depreciating silver was absorbed by India where the mints remained open to the coinage of silver rupees until 1893. The British colonial rulers were very eager to keep the mints open as Indian demand helped to stabilise the price of silver, and its price would have fallen much more steeply otherwise. The automatic depreciation of the Indian silver currency shielded India against the fall in agricultural prices caused by the deflationary effect of the gold standard in the West, but it also had a negative effect. Indian peasants sold their produce for silver which was soon worth much less. This was not a good bargain, but the British colonial rulers did not mind that, they would have kept the mints open for ever if they had not been caught on the horns of a dilemma: the 'home charges' i.e. the tribute which India had to pay to its British rulers, which also included the debt service on India's national debt, had to be paid in gold, but Indian revenue was paid in silver. When they could not make both ends meet, the British closed the Indian mints to the coinage of silver and converted the rupee into a token coin. From 1893 India was on a gold exchange standard, i.e. a standard based on gold but without the circulation of gold coins. This will be explained in more detail in Chapter 9.

The defeat of bimetallism by the 'gold bugs' was practically complete by the end of the nineteenth century. But stability had been achieved at an enormous cost. There was a worldwide depression of agricultural prices in the late nineteenth century due to the deflationary impact of the gold standard. William Jennings Bryan, a candidate for the presidency of the United States, made his famous 'Cross of Gold' speech at the Democratic Party Convention in July 1896. He wished to revive bimetallism in the interest of the American farmers and he told the defenders of the gold standard: 'You shall not press down upon the brow of labour this crown of thorns, you shall not crucify mankind upon a cross of gold'. But Bryan was defeated by the Republican candidate, William McKinley, a defender of the gold standard. Bryan's speech had marked a high point of the debates about the deflationary effect of the gold standard. There had been several committee meetings in Europe considering the question of whether bimetallism should be restored, as gold supply had not been sufficient. But all these controversial debates stopped when South African and other mines yielded enough gold to rescue the monometallic gold standard.

The problem of the scarcity of gold was solved only temporarily at that time though the defeat of bimetallism was final. Of course, in the modern world with its many ways of creating money, the circulation of gold coins was no longer of much importance, but the idea that the currency should have an adequate backing in terms of gold reserves dominated the minds of men and led to a sterilisation of these reserves which militated against the original idea of the gold standard. Only London stuck to the principle of the free flow of gold while in America Fort Knox became proverbial for a practice which was the very opposite of such a free flow. The French later on emulated the Americans and thus London remained the only true supporter of the principles of the international gold standard. Keeping this tendency in mind, the British return to the gold standard in 1925 appears to us as either a heroic endeavour or as folly. We may thus look at the unfolding of events as a tragedy or a tragic comedy with Montagu Norman in the role of a financial Don Quixote.

THE RETURN TO THE GOLD STANDARD

The Bank of England under Norman's leadership was not the only driving force behind the return to the gold standard after the First World War. In fact, the British return to that standard in 1925 did not set the pace but followed developments elsewhere. The United States had never left the gold standard and when the Americans took the initiative of putting Germany once more on the map of international financial relations by means of the Dawes Plan, about which more will be said in the next chapter, Norman obviously felt that Great Britain would be left behind if it did not return to the gold standard immediately. When in 1924 Hjalmar Schacht, the president of the re-established Reichsbank, the German central bank, arrived for his first visit to London in his new capacity, Norman made a point of receiving him at the station, although usually he was not known for such gestures. This was the beginning of a very cordial relationship with Schacht, based on mutual admiration – and one which was very suspect to the French.

In 1925 Norman won his victory, which a perceptive author has described as 'The Norman Conquest of $4.86'. This is an allusion to the prewar dollar parity with the pound which Norman adopted when returning to the gold standard. This parity had acquired an almost irrational sanctity. The French demonstrated three years later that one did not need to stick to it. They returned to the gold standard at one fifth of that parity. The unfortunate Japanese, however, also returned to the gold standard at the prewar parity in 1930. For Norman this obviously had been a matter of prestige, but he regretted it later on and stated that Great Britain had been 'under the harrow' ever since returning to the gold standard at that parity. He had fallen prey to the gold standard orthodoxy according to which prices should have risen in the United States after it had gulped an enormous amount of gold. But as this gold had disappeared into Fort Knox, it did not affect the level of prices in America. The overvalued pound, however, affected the level of prices in Great Britain. Moreover, it had to be maintained at this rate by means of a deflationary monetary policy. As an overvalued currency impedes exports and encourages imports, British industry was badly affected by the 'Norman conquest'.

In his conquest Norman was supported by Benjamin Strong , the powerful Governor of the Federal Reserve Bank of New York. The Federal Reserve system was composed of twelve regional banks of which the one in New York was the most prominent one. The Federal Reserve Board was ex-officio chaired by the Secretary of the US Treasury, but Strong practically dictated monetary policy. Representing the interests of the large New York banks he was an internationalist who worked hard for the return of all European countries to the gold standard. He saw to it that Germany could make the grade by means of the Dawes Plan. He supported Norman and together they helped Italy to join the club. In December 1927 Italy returned to the gold standard by decree, and at a rate which was considered to be high even at that time. Known as 'quota novanta', because approximately 90 lira were to be equivalent to one pound sterling, this rate was very controversial. It could be maintained only by a deflationary monetary policy. However, as has been explained earlier, Strong's successful campaign for the gold standard abroad was in conflict with his policy at home where he sterilised gold and replaced it with Federal Reserve credit.

It was bad enough that the Americans did not play the game according to the rules of gold standard orthodoxy, but to Norman's dismay the French joined the fray in sterilising gold in a big way after 1928. They fixed the gold backing for their currency at the high rate of 35 per cent and gulped gold worth $1 billion from mid-1928 to January 1930. This meant that the Bank of England, which continued to permit the free flow of gold, was now utterly dependent on American and French support. If those two powers had had the good sense to maintain London as a world financial centre as long as they themselves were not in a position to play this role, a trilateral policy could have been adopted which would have supported the world credit structure. Unfortunately a basic disagreement on gold standard policy had emerged at the very time when the intensive cooperation of the three powers would have been most important. The disagreement was about the role of foreign exchange holdings in the interlocking relationship of central banks. In addition to gold, central banks held a large part of their reserves in foreign exchange and this could lead to complications which required deft handling by the central bankers. In 1927 a problem of this kind had been solved with the help of Benjamin Strong, Norman's friend in New York, who dominated the Federal Reserve Board. Norman was proud of this instance of central bank cooperation, but Strong had second thoughts about it. He suggested that these problematic reserves should be reduced and gold reserves should play a more prominent part in the foundation of the gold standard. He felt that instead of holding too much foreign exchange the reserve requirements should be reduced so as not to enhance the competition for gold. For Strong, who could rely on America's large gold reserves, this was a logical suggestion and the French who were just about to acquire a great deal of gold tended to agree with Strong's position. The Bank of England, however, would not benefit from such a plan as it held large foreign exchange reserves and was always under pressure as far as its gold reserves were concerned.

At the back of such disagreements on policy matters there were also political rivalries.The special relationship between Great Britain and the United States was not always so very special, for they were rivals as far as the domination of the global financial network was concerned. The British and the French never really saw eye to eye. Norman hated the French and their monetary policy and was close to the Germans, which was resented by the French. The kind of unofficial link which had joined the Bank of England with the Bank of France when each of them had a Rothschild on its board was a thing of the past. Instead, there was now a stronger unofficial link between London and New York, because Morgan's British partner Grenfell was on the board of the Bank of England. Morgan tried his best to back the Bank of England, but, as will be shown in Chapters 5 and 6, even Morgan was not in a position to fight the depression and save the gold standard. As the crisis approached, Norman became more and more isolated in his valiant attempts at central bank cooperation, which were further jeopardised by the domestic compulsions faced by the Federal Reserve Board after 1927. It tried to curb speculative activity at home by adopting a restrictive monetary policy at the very moment when international cooperation would have demanded the opposite course.

THE INSTRUMENTS OF MONETARY POLICY

In the trying years 'under the harrow' Norman made use of all instruments of monetary policy at his disposal in order to support the gold standard and defend the position of London as a financial centre. The foremost instrument of a central bank in stabilising monetary policy is, of course, the bank rate, i.e the rate at which member banks may discount commercial papers, etc. with the central bank. In the late nineteenth century the Bank of England had kept this rate in general at 3 per cent. To his dismay, Norman had to raise this rate in order to support the overvalued pound after 1925. But for this reason he was very wary with regard to further changes in the rate as this had become a political issue. Industrial interests protested whenever the rate was raised and so did the Labour Party, because a high rate meant an increase in unemployment. Raising or lowering the bank rate is a clear signal to the economy at large, but for this very reason it is a rather problematic instrument. A much more elegant way of regulating money supply is provided by open market operations.

Norman refined this instrument, which had been used even before the war, but it came into greater prominence only in his time and was handled by him very deftly. By buying and selling commercial papers, government bonds and treasury bills the central bank can enhance or reduce liquidity in the money market and it can do this without paying heed to the profit it derives from such transactions, i.e. it can buy or sell such papers even at a loss in the interest of stabilising the money supply. The Bank of England was an unusual central bank as it was privately owned and paid dividends. But making profit was not its first priority. Since the central bank conducts open market operations without being constrained by any consideration of the market price, its interventions are, so to speak, exogenous. The precondition for such open market operations is a broad and deep market, because a narrow one would act as a severe constraint on the effectiveness of such operations, which is why very few national central banks can use this instrument. If the market is broad and deep enough, it also permits sophisticated methods of fine tuning. For instance, the central bank may enter into repurchase agreements, by which it can provide liquidity or contract the money supply almost literally overnight. In earlier times such transactions were limited to fine commercial papers, but those were not readily available in this crucial period, so government bonds and treasury bills were used for this purpose. Treasury bills are issued by the treasury in anticipation of revenue income, thus they must be redeemed within the budget year. They are ideally suited for regulating the money supply by means of open market operations. In the United States the Federal Reserve Board is restricted by legislation to government bonds and bills with regard to its open market operations.

There are two other instruments for regulating the money supply: the fixing of the minimum of reserves to be held by banks and the adjustment of the volume of government expenditure. The former is mostly done by the central bank unless there is specific legislation concerning such reserves; the latter is, of course, entirely in the hands of the government which is, however,

Table 2. 1 Instruments for regulating the money supply

Effect	Interventions of the central bank		Interventions of government	
	Bank rate (discount rate)	Open market operations	Min. reserves of banks	Govt expenditure
Reflation	lower	buy bonds	lower	increase
Deflation	raise	sell bonds	raise	reduce

Note: A condition not stated in this table is that the circulation of the currency remains constant.

supposed to balance its budget – at least according to orthodox prescriptions. Nevertheless, even an orthodox government has some discretion with regard to the timing of its expenditure in the course of the year. For ready reference these various instruments are listed in Table 2.1.

All of these instruments were used by the Bank of England and other central banks. When they were used in defence of the gold standard, they were applied with the effect listed in the last line of the table. The ensuing deflation would depress the price level, discourage investment, increase unemployment, etc. Normally a deflationary policy is followed only for a short period of time so as to correct imbalances and restore stability. But Norman, 'under the harrow', had to pursue a deflationary course for several years. This was a heavy burden anyhow, but as we shall see in the next chapter, there were additional problems which beset the conduct of monetary policy at that time.

3

THE DILEMMA OF WAR DEBTS AND REPARATIONS

The problems which bedevilled postwar monetary policy in several European countries were due to the dilemma of war debts owed by the British, the French and several smaller European countries to the United States, on the one hand, and the reparations which Germany was obliged to pay to France, Great Britain and Belgium on the other. The particular dilemma consisted of the practical financial interrelation between the two types of debts and the theoretical distinction between them on which the United States insisted. The United States had not asked Germany for reparations but was adamant about the payment of the war debts of its allies. Any American appeal for easing the burden of the reparations was accompanied by a statement that this did not mean that the erstwhile allies could expect any reduction of the war debts if they showed generosity as far as the reparations were concerned. This was not sheer obstinacy on the part of the American government, it was a reflection of domestic budgetary compulsions. The debt service of the war debts was an essential part of the American budget: if they were struck off or reduced, the government would have to raise taxes to that extent. In view of the frequent elections, no American politician would dare to risk such an unpopular initiative. In tracing the elements of this dilemma we shall first turn to the dimensions of the debts involved and then discuss the attempts at getting off the horns of this dilemma.

THE DIMENSIONS OF WAR DEBTS AND REPARATIONS

Great Britain, France and several smaller European countries owed war debts to the United States which amounted altogether to $12 billion. The lion's share was that of Great Britain which owed $4.7 billion, France owed $4 billion and the rest was owed by several smaller countries. Great Britain was regarded by the United States as the most affluent debtor, because France owed $3 billion and several other countries owed altogether $8 billion to Great Britain. In other words, Great Britain was more of a creditor than a debtor in this game of war debts. It could, therefore, not hope for lenient treatment by the Americans. In January 1923 Stanley Baldwin, the British finance minister, accompanied by Norman, visited the United States in order to settle the mode of payment of the British war debt. They arrived at a fairly good bargain: the debt was to be repaid within sixty-two years, the rate of interest would be 3 per cent for the first ten years and 3.5 per cent later on. This meant an annual debt service to the tune of $220 to $300 million. This was much less than the debt service on Great Britain's internal war debt, which amounted to £2 billion at an interest rate of 5 per cent. For external and internal war debts the debt service thus amounted to about $650 million (£160 million). This was equivalent, at least in nominal terms, to the amount of capital exported by Great Britain annually before the war.

Whereas the war debts were fixed in rather precise terms, the reparations which Germany was supposed to pay to the allies according to the Treaty of Versailles were not fixed until a committee appointed for this purpose specified an amount of 132 billion gold marks in 1921. This amount was never fully paid but it dangled like the sword of Damocles over Germany. The French were particularly eager to claim their pound of flesh and when the German reparation payments were delayed, they occupied the Ruhr region in order to seize German coal and steel in lieu of debt service. This proved to be a big mistake, because the political damage done in this way was enormous, while the amount of $650,000 which they collected in this way was relatively insignificant. However, in this way the Americans were motivated to enter the scene as honest brokers. They launched the Dawes Plan, which will be discussed in the next section of this chapter. This was a surprising new departure, the more so as the Americans had withdrawn from the European political arena after President Wilson failed to receive the support of the United States Congress for his plans for a new world order centred on the League of Nations, which owed its origin to him, but which the United States refused to join. Isolationism, a venerable American attitude cultivated ever since Thomas Jefferson's warning that the brave New World should not get involved in the troubles of the bad Old World, had triumphed once more.

The political withdrawal did not imply that America also relinquished its role of a powerful creditor. In view of the relevance of the war debts to the American budget, the Americans had to take an interest in the vexed question of the German reparations. Although they emphasised that reparations and war debts were completely different liabilities, they also knew that if Germany defaulted on the reparations, Great Britain and France would be unable to honour their war debts. The Dawes Plan was thus not a feat of disinterested altruism, but an attempt at settling the vexed problem of the payment of reparations in such a way that America could also be assured of the debt service of the war debts.

THE DAWES PLAN: A PRECARIOUS SOLUTION TO THE DILEMMA

The crux of the problem was described by Keynes in 1919 when he analysed *The Economic Consequences of the Peace*. Germany had to earn the money to be paid as reparations to the allies, but they would not give it a chance to do so. Nor could Germany earn that much money by exporting goods to protectionist America. This was a correct diagnosis, but what about the therapy? After the ill-advised French invasion of the Ruhr region, the Americans found the solution: they would lend money to Germany, then Germany could pay the reparations, the British and French could service their war debts, and America would get its money back. It was a virtuous rather than a vicious circle and if nothing intervened, it could go on for a long time. This more or less sums up the Dawes Plan, though it was certainly not articulated in this way and there were several intervening variables which could interrupt the virtuous circle at any time. First of all, the flow of American loans to Germany was not guaranteed in any way: it did actually stop in 1928 and the dilemma then became even more intractable. Furthermore, the day of reckoning was only postponed by this plan, because Germany would now have to service these new debts owed to the Americans in addition to paying reparations to the British and the French. There was another complication: the American loans were not made from government to government, the credit was raised in the American capital market and benefited

34

innumerable German firms and municipalities, etc. which were then also responsible for the debt service. However, for the time being the flow of credit eased the foreign exchange problem and enabled Germany to pay the reparations.

The Dawes Plan did not reduce the total amount of reparations as fixed earlier at 132 billion gold marks ($31.4 billion), but it stipulated that annual payments would be limited to 1 billion gold marks ($240 million) for the time being. This annual payment should then increase to 2.5 billion gold marks ($600 million) by 1929. The Dawes Plan also made provision for a loan based on the assets of the German railroads. This loan amounted to 800,000 gold marks ($190 million), it was raised on the American capital market and was oversubscribed within a few weeks and set the pace for the subsequent flow of American credit to Germany.

Actually it was not so much the comparatively small initial loan which paved the way for the granting of more and more American credit, but the institutional arrangements included in the Dawes Plan. The Reichsbank was restored as an independent central bank and the Americans had the right to appoint half of its board members. In addition there was a permanent American representative stationed in Berlin who had to supervise the proper working of the plan. This was a young banker, Parker Gilbert, about whose activities more will be said in Chapter 6. Hjalmar Schacht, the President of the Reichsbank, found this arrangement quite convenient, because it guaranteed the independence of the Reichsbank from the German government. American supervision by an orthodox banker suited Schacht, as he could use him in order to protect his own position. The confidence of American creditors was, of course, greatly increased by this arrangement.

The virtuous circle established by the Dawes Plan worked very well. The sum total of German reparations paid in the period from 1924 to 1933 amounted to 11.4 billion marks and the sum of German capital imports for this period amounted to 13.5 billion marks. Keynes explained the mechanism which kept this 'virtuous' circle going in the following terms: the payment of reparations had a deflationary impact in Germany and kept interest rates high, this attracted the inflow of capital from abroad. The recipients of the reparations should have experienced the opposite effect, i.e inflation and low interest rates. But as they had to pay their war debts to America, this effect could only be expected over there – and this encouraged American capital export to Germany. The circle appeared to be virtuous rather than vicious, but it could stop at any moment and would then appear to have been vicious.

Another negative aspect of this arrangement was that it was by no means backed by the consensus of all powers concerned. The French, particularly, were facing their own specific dilemma: they were eager to receive reparation payments so they had to be grateful for the Dawes Plan, but on the other hand they wanted to use the reparations as a political handle so as to keep Germany on their leash. The Dawes Plan and the flow of American credit emancipated Germany to a great extent from French influence – and this the French resented.

THE PATTERN OF POLITICAL RIVALRIES

Europe was beset by many rivalries which were also reflected by different attitudes to the reparations. The British were not so keen on the reparations and would have liked to forget about them if some way could have been found to reduce the war debts at the same time. The British had been mostly concerned about the German navy and since that had been wiped out they did not mind befriending Germany. The French, however, were afraid of future German ambitions and wanted to keep Germany down. Their vision of a dangerous Germany proved to be a self-fulfilling prophecy, because their measures enraged the German people and finally contributed to the rise of Hitler. The important conference at Locarno in 1925 in which Germany and the allies arrived at an amicable agreement, which then paved the way for German membership of the League of Nations, unfortunately did not signal the beginning of peaceful cooperation, although this was how it was regarded at the time. Revisionists of all kinds were dissatisfied with the status quo and would raise their heads again when they saw a chance of achieving their aims.

In his analysis of the rise and fall of the great powers Paul Kennedy has established the simple rule that ever since 1500 there was a congruence of economic and political power. But the interwar period is a puzzle for him in this respect. The United States remains an 'offstage' superpower and the actors on the stage all suffer from one ailment or another which prevents them from dominating the scene. It could be added that due to the depression the offstage power was seriously incapacitated economically. Contemporary observers could therefore get the impression that this power would have to remain offstage and that scores could be settled in Europe without American intervention. This was, of course, a fatal illusion, but it took another world war to reveal this fact.

4

WORLD PRODUCTION OF AGRICULTURAL PRODUCE

THE TRENDS OF PRODUCTION AND THE DEMOGRAPHIC TRANSITION

Industrial production stagnated in the interwar period. Capacities installed in the immediate postwar years were never fully utilised and there was industrial unemployment even before the depression. In striking contrast with this there was a significant increase of agricultural production in Western countries and in the output of cash crops around the world. Grain production benefited from progressive mechanisation and the use of chemical fertilisers. In many Western countries agricultural productivity increased by leaps and bounds in this way and agricultural labour could be greatly reduced. The countries of the periphery where many crops were produced by smallholders did not experience such an increase in productivity. The increase in output was usually achieved by extending cultivation rather than intensifying it.

Wheat was overproduced in this way, as will be shown in detail in the subsequent section. A rising population would have consumed more wheat, but instead of increasing, the population of Western countries declined due to the demographic transition. The beginning of such a transition is heralded by a drop in death rates which is then followed by a decline in birth rates. The conditions for such a transition have not yet been fully explained by demographers, but empirical data show that in most Western European countries there was an almost parallel decline of birth rates from about 1900 to 1930. They were reduced by about 50 per cent from 30 to 15 per 1,000 in this period and more or less remained at that level in subsequent years. This reduction of population growth at a time of rising productivity of labour also led to a diversification of the demand for food. Whereas in earlier periods grain products had claimed a major share of family budgets, this was no longer the case in the 1920s.

In contrast with the overproduction of wheat there was no such development as far as rice was concerned. Rice was mostly cultivated by the peasants of Asia: its production will be discussed in detail later in this chapter. Mechanisation and an increase in labour productivity played no role in this field. Moreover, there was as yet no demographic transition in Asia. It had just about started in Japan in the mid-1920s, but birth rates were still at about 30 per 1, 000 in 1930. India's population had stagnated from 1900 to 1920 due to epidemics, but it showed an upswing in subsequent years.

The phenomenon of overproduction was accompanied by a clamour for protection in countries which were threatened by foreign competition. Protection then led to domestic overproduction and added to the international problem. Germany provided a striking example: a protective tariff on wheat of 35 marks per tonne was introduced in 1925, and was raised to 95 marks by 1930. Domestic overproduction then had an impact on the internal price level which remained nevertheless far above the world market price. Domestic overproduction of rice was only noticed in Japan where an embargo on rice imports was imposed in 1928 although these imports had been marginal. The Japanese embargo was therefore initially of no concern to the world rice market.

WHEAT PRODUCTION

Before the First World War the European countries (excluding Russia) had produced on average 35 million tonnes of wheat per year (1903–13). In the same decade the four large exporters of wheat (USA, Canada, Argentina and Australia) had increased their production from 25 to 32 million tonnes and their exports from 7 to 10 million tonnes. The war was a severe blow to European production whereas the four exporting countries mentioned above expanded their production even more and surpassed Europe in this field. The war had pushed up wheat prices: the index for wheat at Liverpool (world market price) increased from 1913 (Index=100) to 1926 (Index=261) in a spectacular way. This was, of course, a strong incentive for the wheat producers. The European countries reached their prewar production level only in

1925, but by that time the four large exporters produced 40 million tonnes and exported 19 million tonnes – about twice as much as before the war. Prices were very volatile under these conditions. The good harvest of 1923, when Europe and the four exporters produced altogether 78 million tonnes, depressed the price level (Index=131), the next year was a bad year (68 million tonnes) and prices rose steeply. Two good years, 1927 and 1928 (82 and 92 million tonnes, respectively) then triggered off a continuous fall in wheat prices. The four large exporters had produced 54 million tonnes in 1928, of which they exported 23 million tonnes. Although 1929 was actually a bad year (77 million tonnes) prices did not rise again. The avalanche could not be stopped any longer.

The credit system had so far operated like a ratchet, financing the storage of surplus wheat so as to prevent a sudden decline of the price level. In 1929 the ratchet broke. Panic sales began as everybody concerned wanted to get rid of stored wheat before the price fell even more. This, of course, precipitated a further fall and by 1931 the wheat price was far below the prewar level (1913=100, 1931=62). The producers responded to this by curtailing their production and their exports, but this took some time. In 1934 and 1935 the four large exporters produced 32 million tonnes, of which they exported 12 million tonnes. In Europe, however, production increased behind tariff walls and reached 40 million tonnes in 1934 and 1935. The taxpayer and consumer had to shoulder the burden of this excessive protectionism. Nationalist propaganda aimed at self-sufficiency helped to justify this policy.

RICE PRODUCTION

Rice was mostly produced as well as consumed in Asia. World rice production dwarfed wheat production, but since all major rice producing countries were at the same time rice consumers, it did not enter the international market to the extent that wheat did. The greatest rice exporter was British India, which still included Burma at that time. The total rice production of British India amounted to 49 million tonnes in 1930 of which only 2 million tonnes were exported. China, including Taiwan, produced 43 million tonnes in that year, Japan 10 million tonnes, and five other Asian countries (the Philippines, Indonesia, Thailand, Indonesia and Korea) produced altogether 22 million tonnes but, with the exception of Thailand, they hardly exported any. However, Thailand's total production amounted to 4.8 million tonnes. Its export capacity was therefore very limited. Of the total Asian rice production of about 124 million tonnes only about 3 million tonnes actually entered the international market. Asian rice production had probably increased by about 10 per cent in the course of the 1920s. This is certainly not evidence of overproduction.

The price of rice was at first not touched by the decline of the wheat price. This was mainly due to the fact that wheat cannot be substituted for rice either in production or in consumption. Wherever rice can be grown it is far more productive and profitable than wheat. Rice eaters are normally so attached to their staple food that they will not switch to wheat even if it is available at a much cheaper price. This is not just a matter of taste but also of the utensils used for preparing food. Accordingly rice prices worldwide retained a fairly high level until the end of 1930 and then suddenly fell so steeply that rice became cheaper than wheat, which was entirely unprecedented.

The event which triggered off this phenomenal fall was a minor one, quite out of proportion with its consequences. Moreover, it was a purely domestic affair, not at all related to the international market. It happened in Japan and in order to understand it one must look at the rather peculiar course of events in that country. After the war Japan had experienced rice riots due to the shortage of this staple food and the high prices, which upset the poor. The government had then followed a policy of encouraging self-sufficiency in rice. Marginal imports from India and Thailand helped to tide over the periods of short supply in the months when the Japanese were waiting for their own rice harvest. In India and Thailand the main rice harvest reaches the market in January. Imports from these countries were then available in Japan in March, whereas the Japanese rice harvest reached the market only in October. In 1928 Japan had attained self-sufficiency and imposed an embargo on the import of Indian rice, initially only for a period of six months, but the embargo was prolonged subsequently. In 1930 there was a very good harvest in Japan and on top of this, it was a period of severe deflation as Japan had just joined the gold standard and immediately felt the difficulty of holding on to it. Deflation and domestic overproduction led to a fall of one-third in the Japanese rice price in a period of only two weeks in October 1930. This was, as has been stated earlier, a purely domestic affair and should have been of no concern to rice traders abroad. But as the international grain traders had just experienced the steep fall in the wheat price, they interpreted this news from Japan as a signal that rice would now follow suit. In November the price of Indian rice collapsed in Liverpool and in January 1931 in Calcutta and Rangoon.

This chain reaction precipitated a fall which was both quicker and steeper than the fall of the wheat price. From about 30 per cent in Japan the fall progressed to more than 50 per cent by the time the shock wave had reached Calcutta – and all this without any change in the supply or demand for rice. The volume of Indian rice exports was not affected by this unfortunate event, only the value had dwindled. The basic economic law that the price is determined by supply and demand did not apply in this case. Keynes could have used this example as another illustration of 'liquidity preference'. All grain merchants from the big ones in the ports to the small ones in the countryside emptied their stores, suspended all credit, stopped forward trading and held on to their cash.

What happened to wheat and rice can serve as a model for the construction of two scenarios. Scenario A refers to crops whose prices declined due to overproduction, and Scenario B to those which experienced a fall in price although there was no over-production and supply and demand remained stable.

SCENARIO A: RUBBER, SILK, COFFEE, TEA AND SUGAR

Asia had a major share in the production of four of these five products. All of them were grown in the 1920s to an ever increasing extent, initially because they fetched a good price and subsequently because the producers concerned continued to grow them while prices were falling in order to protect their income levels – a familiar phenomenon in agriculture. Moreover, most of these crops are grown in plantations whose production can be expanded or curtailed only with a considerable time-lag. It may thus happen that an earlier expansion quite literally bears fruit only at a time when prices decline. The case of rubber fits this type. In 1925 rubber prices increased steeply because there was increasing demand and the expansion of plantations had not yet yielded sufficient output. In 1926, when many rubber plantations reached maturity, prices fell, but since the rubber plantations were in full swing they could not be eliminated all of a sudden. Prices continued to fall while production increased more and more. In fact, 1929 witnessed the peak of world production which amounted to 0.85 million tonnes in that year. Malaya, Indonesia and Sri Lanka, which had jointly produced only 0.25 million tonnes in 1920 had raised their output to 0.8 million tonnes in 1929. When the depression hit the market, rubber prices were already so low that they could not fall much more. They then remained at a low level during the 1930s.

Coffee showed an almost parallel development. In 1924 world production amounted to 1.5 million tonnes, but prices rose and set a signal for further expansion. From 1925 to 1927 prices were volatile and tended to fall. In 1927 output reached 2.1 million tonnes, and the price which had stood at 24 cents per pound had come down to 14 cents by then. The coffee growers reacted to this and reduced production to the 1924 level. The price recovered and reached 19 cents in 1928. This led to renewed optimism and an expansion of production which attained 2.4 million tonnes in 1929. The price plummeted to 10 cents and even another reduction in coffee production did not help. In 1931 a pound of coffee fetched only 6 cents.

Tea would have shared the same fate, but a rather efficient cartel of the three tea producing countries, India, Sri Lanka and Indonesia, forestalled a dramatic fall in the tea price. These three countries had produced 0.28 million tonnes of tea in 1920 and reached 0.38 million tonnes in 1929. The tea price had risen substantially in the early 1920s and had then remained stable for several years until a decline began in 1927. The producers did not at first react to this by a reduction in tea production, but they were forced to do so when they were hit by the depression. They then acted quickly and agreed on reduced export quotas which were firmly controlled by the respective tea associations. In this way they achieved a price rise in 1933 and by 1936 they had once more reached the price level of 1929.

Sugar experienced a much more dramatic rise and fall. World production had been increased by 40 per cent from 1920 to 1929. An enormous price increase in 1923 had stimulated this rapid expansion. But from 1923 to 1933 sugar prices steadily declined with only a brief respite in 1926–27. In spite of this rather steep decline there was no reduction in the production of sugar. A slight reduction was introduced in 1932 but by and large, throughout the 1930s sugar production stood at the same level as in 1929. This was due to the imposition of protective tariffs which in India even led to an expansion of sugar production in the years of the depression. Indonesia, the main sugar exporting country, had expanded production from about 1.5 million tonnes in 1920 to 3 million tonnes in 1929 and had then reduced it to 0.5 million tonnes in 1934 while India reached 3 million tonnes in that year. India did not export sugar, the expansion was entirely due to import substitution at the expense of Indonesia which had earlier exported a great deal of sugar to India.

The production of raw silk, which depends on growing mulberry trees on whose leaves the silkworms feed, experienced an expansion of about the same order as sugar (40 per cent from 1920–29). Production stagnated in the 1930s at the level reached in 1929. Prices had peaked in 1924 and then declined – though not as much as in the case of sugar.

All five products discussed here have one thing in common: their consumption can be curtailed by the consumer in bad times and the demand for them will not substantially increase even if they are sold at a much cheaper price. Their production was expanded in response to rising incomes all over the world, but the absorption capacity was reached very soon and accordingly prices fell long before the depression hit the world market. Supply-side economics does not work in this field. In such cases cartels which impose quotas on the supply so as to stabilise prices are very attractive, but they require strict discipline and can easily be circumvented. The tea cartel could work because only three countries were involved and the producers were limited in number and were well organised. Moreover, there were no protective tariffs or export subsidies as far as tea was concerned and import substitution was impossible. Coffee offered similar possibilities, but as will be shown when discussing Brazil and Columbia, the governments concerned could not agree on a common policy. In the case of tea – as will be discussed later on — the producers actually bypassed their respective governments and then forced their hands. This was unique and could not easily be imitated elsewhere.

SCENARIO B: COTTON

Unlike the cash crops mentioned above, whose use could be curtailed by the consumer, cotton was an essential product, as cotton textiles were the cheapest articles of clothing all over the world. The demand for cotton was therefore very large and its supply very stable. There had been no major changes in cotton production in the 1920s except for some expansion of production in Egypt where a fine variety of fibres was grown which was needed for superior cloth. World production of raw cotton amounted to 5.8 million tonnes, it was only slightly reduced under the impact of the depression (5.2 million tonnes in 1932). The USA contributed about 50 to 60 per cent of world production. Next to the USA India was the major cotton producer (about 1 million tonnes per year), China produced about 0.5 million tonnes and Egypt had expanded its cotton production from 0.27 to 0.38 million tonnes from 1920 to 1929. Cotton exports constituted about 75 per cent of total Egyptian exports and the country was therefore particularly vulnerable in this respect.

In spite of the rather stable relation between supply and demand, cotton prices fell in the USA and in Egypt immediately after the stock market crash of October 1929. But this initial fall amounted to about 20 per cent only. A steeper fall followed from March to September 1930, when the price of cotton dropped from 14.74 to 10.15 cents per pound in the American market. In June 1929 the price had stood at 18 cents, in 1932 it reached its lowest point at 6 cents per pound. This reduction of the price to one-third within three years was more severe than that of most other commodities mentioned so far.

The drop in the price level, which remained depressed for quite some time, caused many American cotton growers to withdraw from this unprofitable business and leave it to the countries at the periphery of the world market. Whereas around 1930 the USA still held a share of 57 per cent of world cotton exports, this was reduced to 42 per cent after 1934. The share of the market yielded by the American growers did not go to the established cotton producing countries but rather to new entrants such as Brazil and Peru which tried to diversify their exports in this way.

It is remarkable that both the rice and the cotton markets registered the steepest price falls and were seriously affected only after the depression had set in, whereas the prices of those commodities which were overproduced had witnessed a decline in prices even before that time. Credit contraction was the major cause of the fall in the rice and cotton prices, plus the self-fulfilling prophecy based on the universal expectation of a fall in prices regardless of supply and demand. The losses caused by this development were enormous. In the summer of 1929, before the depression began, the total value of the world production of raw cotton amounted to about $2.2 billion and of rice to $7 billion. The volume of production remained rather stable after 1929, but the value of the crops was reduced to about one third of their pre-depression value. This meant an enormous loss of income to millions of rice and cotton growers – mostly peasants – because neither rice nor cotton were plantation crops in most of the countries concerned.

The peasants would have been able to endure this calamity much better if the prices of all other goods as well as rents, debt service and tax collection had been reduced to the same extent. But this did not happen. In fact, the prices of industrial goods declined much less than those of agricultural produce. The last section of this chapter will be devoted to a discussion of this problem.

DEBT SERVICE AND THE TERMS OF TRADE

Most peasants in the world were indebted and their debt service had increased as the deflationary policy associated with the maintenance of the gold standard had pushed up interest rates everywhere. It took some time before interest rates declined under the impact of the depression. Moreover, the local money lenders would usually follow a line of high notional interest rates which helped to keep their customers in debt, and variable effective interest rates adjusted to the capacity of the debtors to pay their charges. Under the impact of the depression the money lenders abandoned this system, they stopped lending and wanted to recover their capital. Insolvent peasants then had to part with their savings – usually in the form of gold ornaments – and/or had to sell their land. Much of the gold which thus entered the market flowed to the centres of the world economy and helped to support their currencies and the price level of the industrial goods which they produced. The terms of trade thus shifted against agriculture on the periphery of the world, and the buying power of the people at the periphery of the world market was reduced in this way. The export markets for the products of Western countries were affected by this, and by Japanese competition, as Japan moved in and provided cheap consumer goods to those who could not afford Western products any longer.

Peasant indebtedness became quite a problem for colonial and other governments at the periphery of the world market. These governments tried to control money lenders, provided for debt conciliation, established land mortgage banks, etc. but they hardly ever reduced taxation. As has been mentioned earlier, peasant unrest increased under the impact of the depression. But almost everywhere it was extremely difficult to establish peasant solidarity and rally them to fight for a common cause. People who have to struggle for survival and still have something to lose are not easily persuaded to join a violent rebellion, facing powers which can crush them easily. There was another reason why rural rebellions were rare in spite of the suffering spread by the depression. Political leadership would have had to come from urban people, and they benefited from the shifting of the terms of trade against agriculture. This will be discussed in detail in Chapter 14: the present chapter only provides a background for such a discussion and for the case studies of various countries which suffered under the impact of the depression.

5

THE ORIGIN OF THE
DEPRESSION IN AMERICA

As pointed out in previous chapters, all major factors contributing to the depression can be traced back to the United States of America: the handling of war debts, the sterilisation of gold, a deflationary monetary policy after an expansionist period, protectionism and the overproduction of wheat. All these factors were due to long term developments, but they were accentuated by the sudden crash of the stock market in October 1929 which undermined the world credit system and thus was the proximate cause of the depression. Before turning to the impact of the depression on other countries we must first analyse its origin in America. All other countries imported the depression. But, of course, they also had their indigenous problems which were magnified by it.

An analysis of the causes of the depression in the United States must begin with an examination of the internal economic situation in that country. It was characterised by a very uneven distribution of income, a concentration of capital and a lack of further prospects for productive investment. Instead there was an increase in speculation in the stock market which greatly strained the system of financial intermediation which was still rather disorganised and unregulated. There were also other structural problems of the American economy which have to be kept in mind. In thinking of the United States as a premier industrial country we tend to overlook the fact that around 1930 nearly half of the population lived in rural areas and was either directly or indirectly dependent on agriculture. The farm lobby was of enormous political significance and American fiscal policy was therefore bound to be influenced by that fact. Moreover, 'big government' did not yet exist at that time and thus the effectiveness of fiscal measures was rather limited. The federal government claimed only 2.5 per cent of

48

GNP; another 7.5 per cent was claimed by state and local authorities, but strategic policy measures could only be expected from the federal government. This must be kept in mind when we judge the ability or inability of American presidents to cope with the depression.

In the following sections of this chapter we shall first deal with the economic factors contributing to the depression, then examine the scope of financial intermediation and finally turn to the record of the federal government with regard to crisis management.

INCOME DISTRIBUTION, CAPITAL CONCENTRATION AND THE LACK OF INVESTMENT

There had been a continuous process of polarisation between the rich and the poor in an exceedingly prosperous American society. In the 1920s, 5 per cent of those who received incomes got 30 per cent of the total of all incomes. This meant that the consumption of luxury goods was of major importance. The demand for such goods is much more volatile than mass consumption of essential goods. It is a matter of received wisdom that America led the world in the field of mass consumption, but we should not forget that there were important structural differences in the various phases of American economic development in this respect. The pattern of investment was influenced by such structural differences. In earlier years heavy industry and railway construction had attracted a great deal of investment. The new leading industry of the twentieth century was the car industry, but cars were highly priced consumer goods, the demand for them was limited by the purchasing power of the people and as they were very durable consumer goods there was also the inherent problem of the saturation of the market. Between 1920 and 1928 the number of passenger cars registered in the United States had increased from 8.2 to 21.6 million, while that of trucks had increased from 1 to 3 million. The period of rapid growth was from 1922 to 1926 when registered passenger cars increased roughly by 2 million per year; this rate of growth receded to 1 million per year subsequently. Similarly the number of trucks increased most rapidly from 1922 to 1926 and much less in subsequent years. Production did not yet decline to the same extent. About 4 million cars and trucks were manufactured per year. Some of them were exported, of course, but there must have been a large number waiting to be sold while demand declined. By 1928 there was one car to every six Americans. Considering the uneven distribution of income mentioned earlier, this meant that by 1928 almost everybody who could afford a car had bought one.

Similarly, private construction, which was another important factor of economic growth, seems to have reached a point were further investment was not immediately required. In 1929 $8.9 million was still spent on such construction, but the subsequent deep and long lasting depression in this field seems to indicate that there was no urgent need for new construction. In Great Britain housing construction proved to be a major engine of economic recovery. But in the United States the sum total of investment in private construction for the four years 1933–36 amounted to only about the same amount as that spent in 1929 alone.

A further factor contributing to the reduction of productive investment was the concentration of capital in the hands of the management of giant corporations (Ford, General Motors, the big steel companies, etc.). These corporations did not prove to be very innovative when it came to finding new fields of investment beyond their usual lines of production. Anyhow, such new lines would have had to be in the field of luxury goods. That there was some scope for expansion in this direction was shown by the rapid increase in the import of Japanese silk materials. The sudden decline in the demand for silk then had negative repercussions in Japan.

What else could a rich American buy after having built a big house, acquired one or two cars and dressed his wife in silk? As he was quite aware of the restriction of his own demand, he would be sceptical, too, about finding new avenues of productive investment. Instead of that he used his money for speculation on the stock market. The enormous discrepancy between investment and speculation is obvious when comparing the following figures: new investment in 1925 was $3.5 billion and in 1929, $3.2 billion; the nominal value of shares traded in the stock market in 1925 was $27 billion, in 1929 it was $87 billion.

It should have been clear to everybody concerned that a crash was inevitable under such conditions, but contemporary observers were blissfully unaware of what was going to happen. Even in earlier years income distribution in America had been very inequitable, so why should this be an obstacle to further growth now? America's most distinguished economist at that time, Irving Fisher, a pioneer in the field of econometrics and statistics, was highly optimistic on the eve of the depression. He then lost his entire private property in the depression and would have had to leave his house if his university had not bought it and permitted him to stay on as a tenant. After the event he became wiser and even suggested a theory which anticipated that of Keynes, but his reputation was ruined just as much as his fortune. Fisher's fate showed the surprising lack of economic information and of theories which would have permitted a prediction of the coming crisis. If this was so in his case, we cannot blame ordinary mortals like American presidents, bankers and speculators for not knowing what was going on.

The immediate impact of the depression was very severe. Non-farm employment dropped from 35.6 million in 1929 to 27.9 million in 1932, then increased very slowly until it stood at 36 million in 1937. Total private domestic investment, which had amounted to $16.2 billion in 1929, surpassed this level only by 1941. In the meantime it receded to very low levels (e.g. $3.3 billion in 1934). The net income of farmers also fell very steeply and recovered only very slowly. Net income from an average American farm amounted to $945 in 1929 and dropped to $304 in 1932; from this lowest point it recovered by slow steps almost to its previous level in 1937, after which it fell once more and surpassed the 1929 level only in 1941. As stated before, rural inhabitants constituted nearly half the American population and their purchasing power was so severely reduced by the depression that they could not be expected to contribute to an economic upswing.

FINANCIAL INTERMEDIATION: BANKERS AND SPECULATORS

Banking had expanded by leaps and bounds in nineteenth-century America. There were local banks everywhere which catered to the specific needs of their customers. Large New York banks like J.P. Morgan's had acquired enormous power and could not be controlled. It was only in 1913 that the Federal Reserve Board was created. Its statutes were very complicated so as to strike a delicate balance between central control and local autonomy. There were twelve regional central banks under the Federal Reserve Board, privately owned by the banks in their area which could discount commercial papers with them. By raising or lowering the discount rate these banks could regulate the money supply. The apex of the system, the Federal Reserve Board, consisted of members nominated by the American president. The respective legislation had been introduced in order to tame the powerful New York banks, but it was soon evident that the New York central bank was the most important one and that its governor was more powerful than the Federal Reserve Board.

The members of the twelve regional central banks were bankers recruited from the member banks and therefore they behaved exactly as other local bankers would do. They knew next to nothing about the problems of money supply. They should have raised the discount rate in an upswing and lowered it in a recession so as to reflate the economy, but they did the very opposite. They eagerly discounted good commercial papers at low interest rates when they were presented by their members and when they did not get good papers, due to a recession, they hesitated to discount them and demanded high interest rates. A critic of the system, Lauchlin Currie, who published his book on money supply in the United States in 1934, called this behaviour of the bankers 'perverse flexibility'. He stated that the American central bankers had no idea of monetary policy and did not even know how to define credit. They did not distinguish between deposits and credit in analytical terms and thus they did not know what the supply of money which they were supposed to control really was. The only thing they knew was how to evaluate the commercial papers offered to them for discounting. The predicament of these bankers was accentuated by the fact that in the course of the 1920s the quantity and quality of commercial papers presented to them receded. The Bank of England had the same problem, but in a brisk trade in treasury bills and government bonds it found an alternative which enabled it to control money supply by open market operations. The decline of the volume and value of fine commercial papers in America was caused by the increasing tendency of resorting to the stock market rather than to the banks for raising capital. The stock market was autonomous and could not be controlled by the Federal Reserve Board. The banks participated in stock market business only to the extent that they would provide credit to their clients for buying shares. If the central banks wanted to curtail this business by raising discount rates they could not help affecting the whole credit market in this way. The speculators, however, were not discouraged by higher interest rates as they expected to make a profit by buying and selling shares, otherwise they would not have been in the game at all.

The impotence of the central banking system was in striking contrast to the power of holding companies which mushroomed in those years before the great crash. Instead of investing in new production, the holding companies bought up existing plants and raised the capital for this in the stock market. As long as they paid dividends and their stock was rising, the speculators did not care to look behind the façade of these holding companies. These dubious transactions became even more complicated because of the fact that both the holding companies and their shareholders borrowed money from the banks, which demanded from their clients only a fraction of the value of the shares which they deposited with them, asking them to pay up only when stock prices were falling. The whole edifice was like a set of houses of cards which mutually supported each other. As long as stocks were rising the construction was fine, but a sharp fall in the prices of shares was bound to bring it all down at once.

When the stock market crashed in October 1929 nobody could stop the avalanche. J.P. Morgan and his crew tried to stem the tide by offering higher prices on the floor of the stock exchange. This was a brave but utterly futile gesture. Only the Federal Reserve Board could have intervened effectively. It actually did so in order to stabilise the credit market, but it was a halfhearted attempt. It should have embarked immediately on a reflationary policy, but instead of this it practised 'perverse flexibility' with a vengeance. It reduced the money supply 'automatically' and thus caused a sharp deflation which transmitted the impact of the crash to all sectors of the economy and thereby turned the crash into a depression. This is where Milton Friedman and his monetarist colleagues come in, with their severe criticism of the Federal Reserve Board which had been formulated in much the same way by Lauchlin Currie. But as our analysis has shown, the Federal Reserve Board could not have acted more wisely under the conditions prevailing at that time. Even if Irving Fisher had been in charge of the board, he would have probably acted in the same way – not to mention the conservative bankers who were actually in charge at that time. Fisher later on proposed a debt–deflation theory which has been referred to in Chapter 1. This theory explained very well what had happened, but that was with the benefit of hindsight.

Moreover, while monetary forces do influence the 'real economy' there is a limit to their effectiveness and they usually need some time to make themselves felt. The very essence of monetarist theory is the steadying effect of long term monetary policy. It is not suited for a quick fix, but, of course, it provides a powerful analytical tool for a post mortem examination of what went wrong.

THE EXTERNAL ECONOMIC RELATIONS OF THE UNITED STATES

With its large home market and its huge rural population the United States were essentially an inward looking country with very little concern about the outside world. The contribution of foreign trade to its GNP was comparatively small, but its position as a major international creditor made it the most important factor in the world market. Just like Great Britain before the First World War, the United States had a positive balance of payments with the rest of the world after the war. This was mostly due to its capital export but also to debt service of the war debts. Great Britain had normally had a negative balance of trade with the rest of the world, for which it could compensate by means of 'invisibles' which swelled its balance of payments. The United States had a positive balance of trade, mostly due to its ingrained protectionism which had prevailed even before the First World War. Therefore it was extremely difficult for America's debtors to earn money by exporting goods so as to cope with their debt service. Accordingly more and more gold had to be shipped to the United States. If this gold had increased the American money supply instead of disappearing into Fort Knox, the ensuing inflation would have relieved the burden of debtors within the United States and stimulated economic activity. But the American government was dead set against an inflationary policy and in this way put a great deal of pressure on its debtors abroad whose gold it absorbed, thus deflating their economies. As has been pointed out earlier, gold sterilisation was also enhanced by the monetary policy of the Federal Reserve Board which was devoted to price stability. This policy was more successful in preventing a rise in prices but less so when it was necessary to counteract a fall in prices.

The depression accentuated all this even more. The value of

monthly imports into the United States, which had amounted to about $400 million for several months before October 1929, receded to $300 million in January 1930 and even further to $200 million in the autumn of that year. The Smoot–Hawley Act of 1930, which increased protective tariffs, was responsible for this further drop in imports. It was seen as a purely domestic measure to prevent the further fall of prices, but it provoked immediate retaliation by other governments and contributed to the contraction of international trade. It encouraged the trend towards autarky all over the world and sent the wrong signal around the globe. It was in keeping with this trend that Keynes later constructed his model for the revival of the economy on the basis of a closed national economy. This reflected contemporary reality. Moreover, a model which relies on fiscal measures rather than on a revival of international trade is quite naturally based on the assumption of a closed national economy. Great Britain followed the American example in the years after 1931, but it prevented India from following this path, as we shall see in Chapter 9.

The American quest for autarky set the pattern for the rest of the world. This quest was, so to speak, the economic counterpart of political isolationism. It would have been in keeping with such a position to relinquish the position of creditor to the world, but this America did not do. President Hoover only made a small concession to the plight of the depressed world by announcing a moratorium on the debt service of war debts, linking it with the demand that the beneficiaries of this moratorium should also suspend their demands for reparations for the same period. Unfortunately the period concerned was only one year. Probably Hoover had hoped that by that time the depression would be over and everybody could return to business as usual. Interestingly enough, this moratorium for the first time linked the war debts with the reparations, a link which the Americans had always denied. It would have been in keeping with this new approach to propose a debt swap. Great Britain and France would give up their reparation claims and in return Germany would pay their war debts to the United States. This aspect will be discussed later on when we are dealing with Germany. The United States did not want to cancel these war debts because they would have had to raise taxes at home, as has been explained earlier. Raising taxes would have been an even more unpopular measure in the midst of the depression when the goverment was expected to slash taxes and also to stimulate the economy by means of federal spending. Under those circumstances the Hoover Moratorium was almost an act of heroic altruism – at least it was in complete contrast to Hoover's approval of the Smoot–Hawley Act.

ROOSEVELT'S DOMESTIC AND FOREIGN ECONOMIC POLICY

When Roosevelt replaced Hoover in January 1933 everybody expected a new departure in economic policy although Roosevelt had been remarkably vague in his election campaign about what he intended to do. Later interpretations of prominent economists have tended to highlight the boldness or even ruthlessness of Roosevelt's new departure. It has been said that he introduced an entirely new economic regime, but he has also been blamed for wrecking the World Economic Conference which had been planned when Hoover was still in office. It was convened in London in June 1933 and was supposed to coordinate the various exchange rates which had emerged after the British and others had abandoned the gold standard. Roosevelt did not attend the conference and finally sent a bombshell message which practically put an end to its deliberations. But a close-up of Roosevelt's actions in 1933 shows a rather different picture of his political conduct.

Roosevelt's main support came from the American farmers who badly needed higher prices for agricultural produce, which could only be achieved by a devaluation of the dollar and a dose of imported inflation which would reflate the American economy. So even before Roosevelt took office in January 1933 there was widespread speculation that he would opt for devaluation and abandon the gold standard. He had neither promised nor denied that and therefore devaluation became a self-fulfilling prophecy much in the same way as in South Africa in 1932. As a major gold producing country South Africa was under no compulsion to abandon the gold standard, but after the British had established that precedent, there was a great deal of talk about South Africa following suit, which it finally did under this self-generated compulsion. Roosevelt's silence was interpreted as his being in favour of devaluation, and the time between his election in November 1932 and his taking office in January 1933 was rife with rumours which caused many people to withdraw their bank deposits.

By the time he assumed office, Roosevelt was faced with a wave of bank failures. Bank holidays were declared and instead of going ahead with devaluation, Roosevelt posed as a champion of stability and bank deposits increased once more. He was now caught on the horns of a dilemma. The farmers were breathing down his neck while the banks needed stability. Financial interests abroad were speculating against the dollar. Roosevelt imposed a gold export embargo and finally took the plunge on 19 April 1933 when the British and the French prime ministers were on board ship on their way to America. They were surprised by the news, which made consultations even more important to avoid a slanging match of competitive devaluations. The French were under particular pressure as they remained wedded to the gold standard. The Tripartite Agreement, which emerged three years later at the time when the French left the gold standard, should have been concluded in 1933. Roosevelt was even prepared to settle for a 15 per cent devaluation of the dollar at that time and wanted to establish a joint stabilisation fund so as to coordinate the exchange rates. But the British and the French could not accept his suggestions, due to domestic pressures of their own, and thus the chance was missed. This did not increase Roosevelt's enthusiasm for the World Economic Conference which was to follow soon and which was devoted to the same problem he had discusssed in vain with the two prime ministers. His bombshell message to the conference must be seen in this context. He admonished the other powers that they should put their houses in order before expecting anything from him. He refused to consider American participation in any stabilisation plan. His rude reaction was precipitated by domestic concerns as rumours emanating from the conference had raised fears that there would be a return to deflationary policies and prices began to fall in the American market. This was the last thing that Roosevelt could put up with, in view of the needs of his farmers. He did not want to interfere with the fall of the dollar unless it declined excessively. Domestic interests were more important than international stability.

In addition to devaluation, Roosevelt also tried to help the farmers by means of special legislation to solve the problem of overproduction. The Agricultural Adjustment Act of 1933 helped the farmers in the short run as they were paid for restricting production by reducing the acreage they cultivated. But the act did not prevent them from intensifying production on the land which they were permitted to cultivate. This would again lead to over-production and depress the price level, but in the short run the farmers benefited from having it both ways, i.e. getting paid for the land they did not cultivate and yet making money on the crops they produced on the rest of their land. They had good reasons for supporting Roosevelt once more in the elections of 1936.

He was less successful in pleasing the industralists who were initially in favour of his National Industrial Recovery Act of 1933, but then resented the bureaucratic regulations introduced by it and the wages it guaranteed to labour. The act was struck down by the Supreme Court in 1935. Having won the elections in 1936 Roosevelt showed a different face. He tried to balance the budget and raised taxes. He had always been in favour of fiscal orthodoxy, and having been assured of a second term he wanted to return to it with a vengeance. But in this way he only precipitated a renewed depression in 1937–38, which has been mentioned above. Farmers were affected by it as their incomes dropped once more and investors also felt discouraged. Total private investment, which had stood at $11.8 billion in 1937 dropped to $6.5 billion in 1938. The number of non-farm unemployed rose by about 30 per cent from 1937 to 1938. Roosevelt was lucky that he had just won an election and did not need to face another one until 1940, for by that time farm income was high, investment had increased and unemployment had dropped once more to the 1937 level.

Looking back at Roosevelt's much admired 'New Deal' we may say that most of it was of rhetorical rather than practical value and that his devaluation of the dollar was perhaps his most successful measure. His return to fiscal orthodoxy at the beginning of his second term was a bad blunder and his cavalier treatment of the rest of the world was intolerable. But in view of the domestic situation with which he had to cope this attitude is understandable. It meant, of course, that America could not provide constructive leadership to the world at a time when this would have been of utmost importance.

6

THE TRANSMISSION OF THE CRISIS TO EUROPE

The depression was transmitted from America to Europe in 1930. The stock market crash of October 1929 did not have an immediate effect on Europe. On the contrary, financial circles could heave a sigh of relief as they were no longer threatened by the rush of funds to New York. Discount rates which had been raised to counteract that flow could be lowered once more and this eased the strain on European financial markets. From 1925 to the beginning of 1929 the discount rate of the Bank of England had stood at about 4.5 per cent. By September 1929 it had been raised to 6.5 per cent. Immediately after the crash it was reduced to 6 per cent. It was then lowered bit by bit until it stood at 2.5 per cent in May 1931. In France a new generous programme of state expenditure was announced only a few weeks after the crash. But this was not done in wise anticipation of the impending crisis, but only because France had consolidated its currency and was in a very comfortable financial position. It could afford such a programme now, and nobody thought of a crisis.

Germany faced an impending bankruptcy at that time which was entirely unrelated to the events in America. The German government was under political pressure to cut taxes, but on the other hand it could no longer place long term government bonds and thus depended on short term credit. In this context the lowering of the discount rate after the crash was very welcome to the government. In subsequent years Germany faced a crisis of a special kind which will be analysed in the respective section of this chapter. At this stage these statements may suffice to show that the crash of 1929 did not mark the beginning of the depression in Europe. The mechanism of the transmission of the depression was much more complex. Europe was affected only after a

59

considerable time lag. In order to reconstruct the process of transmission we shall present four case studies: Great Britain, Germany, France and Sweden, the latter so as to illustrate a very special instance of successful crisis management.

GREAT BRITAIN

Great Britain was plagued by a permanent crisis in the 1920s, which was due to a conflict of interests among three major groups: the City of London as the centre of world finance, British industry, and labour. The City had reached its aim of returning to the gold standard which enabled it to transact international business along the lines of prewar times. The return to the gold standard at the prewar parity in 1925 had been a mistake, as it forced the City to adopt a deflationary course so as to support the overvalued pound. This affected British industry both with regard to its export position and its access to credit. German and Belgian competitors captured important parts of traditional British export markets, and high interest rates prevented new investment urgently required for bringing industrial equipment up to date. The City did not show much interest in the credit problem of British industry as it was fully occupied with its international transactions. Labour had clamoured for higher wages and had got them. This led to constant complaints from industrialists that high wages enhanced the cost of production and reduced the international competitiveness of British products. The same complaint could be heard in Germany in those days.

Higher wages could be justified by an enhanced productivity of labour, but it was an open question to what extent the increase in productivity really matched the rise in wages. In Great Britain this was doubtful as both conservative industrialists and organised labour looked askance at rationalisation aimed at greater productivity. When unemployment increased in an environment of reduced investment and high wages, the government had to hand out the dole to larger numbers of workers and this could only be paid by raising taxes, which discouraged investment even more. This is how the industralists portrayed the vicious circle in which Great Britain had been caught even before the depression. At that time the deflationary policy of the Bank of England had already made matters worse. When the bank had to raise its discount rate at a time of intense American speculation, the tension increased.

The lowering of the discount rate after the crash could not immediately change the situation, especially as the Labour Party had come to power in 1929 and that had increased the pessimism of the industrialists. The Labour Party could not be expected to sanction a cut in the dole, but in its fiscal and monetary policy the Labour government strictly adhered to the orthodox 'treasury view'. It did this for a very good reason, because it feared that an inflationary policy would reduce the real wages of labour. This showed a concern for the position of those workers who were still employed, although the unemployed might have got jobs under an inflationary regime. But under the conditions prevailing at that time, it was safer to protect the real wages of labour as well as the dole for the unemployed.

In 1930 there were not yet any definite signs of an impending depression. Everybody was confident that business would continue as usual. At that time there was an increase in financial transactions which appeared to be very profitable but which were bound to enhance the financial vulnerability of Great Britain. Even the Bank of England knew very little about these transactions which were caused by the withdrawal of the United States from granting credit to European countries. The British bankers tried to capture this market and earned a good deal of money by accepting short term foreign deposits and lending money at high interest rates. This worked very well as long as short term money from abroad flowed into London and confidence in the British banks remained unshaken. The slightest loss of confidence would destroy this edifice, as short term deposits would then be withdrawn while British bankers could not call in the money which they had lent for longer terms abroad. When in 1931 bank failures on the European continent became the order of the day, the Bank of England was unable to serve as a lender of last resort. Montagu Norman, the Governor of the Bank of England, tried his best to stem the tide, but by desperately trying to take on the task of a lender of last resort he actually made matters worse. This happened because he had no idea of the dimensions of the transactions of the British banks described above, and therefore did not know about the enormous boomerang which was about to hit the City of London.

The problem started with the bankruptcy of the Creditanstalt in Vienna whose plight was caused to some extent by French interests. The French certainly did not try to save the Creditanstalt

61

and hated Norman for supplying an emergency Bank of England credit to it. The French were eager to sabotage the plan of a customs union between Austria and Germany at that time and Norman's intervention disturbed their political design. Norman, on the other hand, tied his hands by bailing out the Creditanstalt, because when the German Reichsbank failed soon after he had no means to provide another emergency credit. All he could do was to bring about a standstill agreement by which foreign creditors pledged not to withdraw money from Germany for the time being. The German government backed this up by the introduction of stringent foreign exchange controls which were not directed against foreign creditors but against German citizens who had transferred much of their money abroad, as they did not trust the German economy any longer. The combination of the standstill agreement and German exchange controls led to a run on London by foreign creditors. They feared that their liquidity would be impaired and withdrew money from London where it was still freely available. Since the British banks could not withdraw their money from Germany they were soon at the end of their tether and looked to the Bank of England as their lender of last resort. Norman organised American and French loans to the Bank of England, but this money disappeared as quickly as it had come in. At this stage one would have expected a substantial raising of the discount rate by the Bank of England, but this was impossible for political reasons. The Labour government was on the brink of disaster, but it was not the government but Norman who collapsed, and went off to the United States to recover his health.

The Labour government did not survive, however, although Prime Minister Ramsay Macdonald remained in office, heading a national government in which the Conservatives emerged as the senior partner. Keynes had written to Macdonald in August 1931, advising him that the game was up and that Great Britain should abandon the gold standard and head a new sterling bloc. This was beyond the prime minister's comprehension. The actual decision for abandoning the gold standard was arrived at a few weeks later at the Bank of England in consultation with Morgan and his London partner, Grenfell, because Morgan was the greatest private creditor of the Bank of England. The text which the British government used to explain why it had abandoned the gold standard was to a large extent drafted by Morgan's staff in New York, as he was shooting grouse in Scotland at the time, but rushed to London for one of his extremely rare encounters with the press. He expressed his full confidence in the British government and in the Bank of England. This he had to do in his own interest so as to prevent a run on his bank, but he was later very much disappointed by Norman who paid the Bank of England's debts to foreign governments in gold but left Morgan with his sterling bonds which were now worth very much less than before.

Norman resumed his work at the Bank of England immediately upon his return from the United States. He pretended that he had not been informed about the departure from the gold standard and that he was disgusted with it. This was probably a white lie to save his face, but his staff kept mum and guarded the secret for all time to come. Now free from the shackles of the gold standard with which he had fettered himself, Norman embarked on a national monetary policy rather than an international one. He lowered the discount rate step by step until it stood at 2 per cent, and he maintained it at that level until the Second World War. Actually, the discount rate was no longer important after the government created a new instrument, the Exchange Equalisation Account, which provided enormous scope for open market operations that dwarfed those with which Norman had worked in the 1920s. As its name indicates this account held foreign currency reserves. It was nominally under the control of the treasury, but was actually operated by Norman at the Bank of England. He could buy and sell large amounts of government bonds and thereby determine money supply as well as the exchange rate of the pound which was freely floating at that time and had depreciated by about 30 per cent.

After lowering the discount rate Norman was successful in landing another great coup: the conversion of the national war debt. War bonds had an interest rate of 5 per cent. The holders of these bonds were persuaded to part with them in exchange for new ones at 3.5 per cent interest but with a longer maturity. The treasury was very keen on this conversion, because the war debt amounted to £2 billion, and saving 1.5 per cent interest on this amount meant a budget relief to the tune of £30 million. Nobody believed that Norman could do the trick. There were not only innumerable small bondholders, but there were also some big banks which held large amounts of these war bonds. The head of the bank which held the biggest amount was particularly recalcitrant as he had been Norman's adversary for some time. Norman offered to buy that bank's holdings of war bonds at the market price, a generous offer which could not easily be rejected. The banker accepted and after this strategic victory the conversion plan could proceed unhindered.

But it was not only Norman's clever management which improved the chances of British monetary policy. There was also the enormous flow of gold from India which will be discussed later on (see Chapter 9). This flow was used to increase British gold reserves and to reflate the currency. The currency in circulation had amounted to £2.1 billion between 1929 and 1931, in the last quarter of 1932 it stood at £2.3 billion and by the end of 1936 it had increased to £2.6 billion, i.e. an increase of about 25 per cent within four years. This stimulated investment and especially private construction which was the most important contribution to British recovery from the depression.

The British banks survived the crisis fairly well. Their real profits fell sharply from 1929 to 1931, but they transferred some of their hidden reserves and published nice balance sheets which kept their shareholders happy. The capacity for survival of the British banks had been strengthened by mergers prior to the depression. In this way the large clearing banks had teamed up with exchange banks and those engaged in business overseas which would have been less equipped to weather the storm on their own. Furthermore, there had been a shift of focus in overseas banking activities, South America had receded and South Africa had become more prominent in British banking business. From 1931 to 1934 the real profits of British banks rose steeply and after 1933 they exceeded their published profits once more.

Actually, devaluation and reflation would have been sufficient to overcome the depression, but on top of this Great Britain had also opted for protectionism. The respective act was passed in November 1931. Before Great Britain had abandoned the gold standard and thus devalued its currency, protectionism and devaluation had been discussed as alternative measures of crisis management. Keynes and other economists thought that there was no need to opt for protectionism after one had already opted for the other alternative. But political pressure had gathered such momentum that protectionism could not be stopped any longer. Many British industries which had priced themselves out of the market internationally now wanted to be sure of their control of the home market. Export industries as well as the Labour Party were in favour of free trade, but the Labour Party had lost power and was overruled by the protectionist interests in the Conservative Party. The abandonment of the principle of free trade and the recourse to protectionism was a global trend which Great Britain could not resist for any length of time. America had set a precedent which was followed by one nation after another. When Roosevelt devalued the dollar and the impact of the devaluation of the pound was reduced in this way, the protectionists triumphed. Those who had advocated the measure in the first place could proclaim that they had been right, but they also gained new converts. Keynes displayed mercantilist tendencies, as will be shown later on, when reporting his views concerning Argentinian beef and British industrial products.

In discussing British neo-mercantilism we should not forget the Ottawa Conference of 1932 which served the purpose of lining up the British Empire as a mercantilist unit. The basic principle of this conference can be characterised by the paradoxical term 'multiple bilateralism'. Great Britain declared which goods of each specific empire country it would admit free of duty and which British goods it would expect to have similar access to the respective country. Some of these arrangements were very clever. For instance, India was given free access for ten items, mostly ores and raw produce, for which the British would probably not have found cheaper suppliers anyhow, but in return there was a long list of British industrial products which were expected to have access to the Indian market.

GERMANY

There were many similarities between German and British experience in the postwar era with the exception of the fact that there was no parallel in Great Britain to the staggering inflation from which Germany suffered in 1923. This fateful event had both negative and positive sides. The negative effect was that all savings were wiped out, which created a great deal of social injustice; the positive side was that debts as well as the internal government debt were cleared in this way. This paved the way for new investment. But the reparations which France and Great Britain claimed from Germany could not be wiped out in this way. They remained a permanent problem and one to which the German government had to adopt a highly ambivalent attitude.

On the one hand it had to uphold the creditworthiness of Germany, on the other, it had to agitate against reparations when faced with internal opposition. Gustav Stresemann, the foreign minister who led Germany back into the arena of world affairs, raised this ambiguity to the level of a fine art. He was very much concerned with creditworthiness, because beginning in 1924 American credit became of major importance for German postwar reconstruction; on the other hand he hoped that the American creditors would in their own interest try to get Germany off the hook of reparations.

The Dawes Plan, which has been discusssed in Chapter 4, had opened the doors to American credit for Germany. Under this plan a special American representative posted in Germany was supposed to monitor the prompt payment of reparations. This representative, Parker Gilbert, was a young banker who was close to Benjamin Strong, the powerful New York central banker. He took his job very seriously and wanted to make the Dawes Plan work. This made him a natural ally of the French, whereas the Germans had hoped that he would be their ally and would help them to prove that they could not be expected to pay the reparations. In fact, German politicians soon came to fear that Gilbert's negative judgement of their policies would stop the flow of American credit. As a conservative banker Gilbert insisted on a balanced budget and rejected a policy of easy money. Actually, he was quite right within his terms of reference. Reparations could be paid best whenever Germany adopted a deflationary policy which would reduce the demand for imports and leave Germany with an export surplus available for the payment of reparations. But as German experience in 1926 showed, monetary contraction would cause a rise in unemployment, which stood at 22 per cent in that year. No German government that depended on parliamentary support could have followed such a deflationary policy for any length of time.

Gilbert was not unaware of the German predicament, caused by the vicious circle of reparations and war debts. If Great Britain and France had been free to spend the reparations they received on buying goods from Germany, this would have stimulated the German economy, but they were not free to do so because they had to pay interest on their war debts to the United States. Therefore Gilbert conceived of a plan to cut the Gordian knot: he suggested that the Germans should pay the interest on the allies' war debts and the allies should cancel their reparations claims. Gilbert also hoped that as part of that bargain the United States would reduce the period of servicing the war debts, which was supposed to run over sixty-two years. The French were not really interested in this plan, because it would have meant them losing the political lever which the reparations provided. The Young Plan, which replaced the Dawes Plan in 1929, did not solve the problem either, it just reduced the reparation payments. The war debts remained as they were. In 1932 Germany defaulted on the reparations and in 1934 the allies defaulted on their war debts. But when the depression hit Germany the problem had not yet been solved in this way and Brüning, whose position will be described later on in this chapter, adopted the course mentioned above, i.e. deflation with rising rates of unemployment in order to demonstrate once and for all that Germany could not pay the reparations without resorting to such masochistic policies. This, of course, greatly enhanced the impact of the depression at that time and paved the way for the rise of Hitler – which was certainly not Brüning's intention.

The Weimar Republic had tried its best to project the image of a modern welfare state and in doing so it had incurrred a great deal of expenditure which led to increasing taxes and indebtedness. When in 1928 the flow of American credit stopped and unemployment increased, the industrialists clamoured for a cut in taxes. At the same time indebtedness had reached such a level that no further government bonds could be placed and the political system was severely strained. The British precedent of forming a national government in which the Labour Party was, of course, in a very weak position, could not be followed in Germany, because the degree of political polarisation was so high that coalitions would not work any longer. For such an eventuality the Weimar constitution provided the unfortunate alternative of a government appointed by the president which was only tolerated by the legislature. Instead of laws to be passed by parliament the government drafted ordinances to be promulgated by the president, and the government continued in office as long as the president supported it. The government headed by Heinrich Brüning served under these conditions from March 1930 to May 1932. This fairly long tenure was quite remarkable in such difficult times. The reasons for this were not very positive ones. There was a political stalemate which could not be overcome and therefore nobody wanted Brüning's job.

Mancur Olson has coined the term 'distributional coalitions' for the pressure groups which emerge when economies do not grow but shrink, and the cake which has to be shared becomes smaller and smaller. These coalitions then try to defend their respective shares. They rarely come up with new ideas and at best arrive at some kind of truce, but at worst they may block the political process altogether. However, in this way they also become impotent. It was Brüning's fate to handle such a situation, but it also provided him with a chance to remain in office. Unfortunately he did not use this chance for any bold departure. He followed an orthodox policy of balancing the budget. His monetary policy was very deflationary. He tried to uphold the creditworthiness of Germany and to pay the reparations in order to arrive at a settlement. Recent critics of Brüning's unimaginative behaviour have argued that he should have left the gold standard, at least after the British had done so. Keynes, who wanted Germany to join the new sterling bloc, had given this sound advice. However, British official opinion at that time was not that abandoning the gold standard was a bold and forward looking policy but rather that it was a disaster. Unofficial British invitations to take the plunge were thus not very convincing to Brüning. Moreover, the French threw spanners into his works and stymied his foreign policy initiatives such as the customs union with Austria. He had to face the financial crisis of 1931, which has been described above, and which he mastered by imposing strict exchange controls which enabled Germany to remain on the gold standard. Since the German people were highly sensitive to any sign of inflation, he stuck to the gold standard in order to protect monetary stability. In fact, the new regime of exchange controls could be used to shore up the government's position while facing disaggregated interests. Political parties are supposed to aggregate interests, but as this process was blocked in Germany at the time, the only alternative was to deal with disaggregated interests separately. For instance, under the exchange control regime the government could please exporters by granting subsidies to them and permitting them to use some of their export earnings for imports, while importers would be granted specific licences, etc. Trade relations with foreign countries reflected this new regime. Bilateral clearing house agreements were made with many countries which had to buy as much from Germany as Germany bought from them. This policy, which began under Brüning, was later continued under Hitler. In the late 1930s about 80 per cent of German foreign trade was conducted in this way. The Soviet Union emerged as a particularly important partner of Germany in the depression years. The mercantilist regime which Germany evolved as a solution to the problems of the depression was very well organised. But it was not unique to Germany. The reference to the Ottawa Conference has shown that Great Britain had also taken steps in this direction, but having cast off the shackles of the gold standard, Great Britain was in a more comfortable position. Germany retained the gold standard but neutralised it by its full fledged mercantilist regime.

While Brüning was still managing to stay in power with his ordinances and controls, Hitler had started a new process of interest aggregation by rallying all dissatisfied elements and providing a rather vague common denominator for their aspirations. Brüning, who was a competent administrator but no resourceful politician, could not cope with this new challenge. He had earlier underestimated Hitler whom he regarded as a vulgar man who would never have a chance of getting anywhere in German politics. He was now flabbergasted by Hitler's success at the polls, but did not know how to tackle him. At this juncture the role of President Paul von Hindenburg became of crucial importance. He was a hero of the First World War, a conservative with no particular political aptitude, but he was very popular among a broad spectrum of German citizens who voted for him when he stood for re-election in March 1932. Hitler, who had stood against Hindenburg, was defeated by him by a big margin. One might have expected that Hindenburg would now back Brüning to the hilt, but he listened instead to the advice of a conservative clique which thought that a move further to the right was required in order to steal Hitler's thunder. Brüning was ditched, but the stratagem of the conservative clique did not work and finally Hindenburg stooped to requesting Hitler to form a government. The president's advisers felt that Hitler could be a useful tool in controlling the masses and protecting the interests of German capitalists. But the tool soon got out of control and became a dictator, and when Hindenburg conveniently died in August 1934, Hitler assumed his office, too.

The German capitalists did well under Hitler's rule. Hjalmar Schacht, Hitler's economic tzar, was a well known conservative central banker whom they could trust. He slowly reflated the economy and otherwise made use of all the instruments which had already been put in place. Hitler's claim to fame as the man who overcame the depression in Germany was actually due to Schacht's steady pursuit of a policy which had been inaugurated by Hitler's predecessors. Hitler backed Schacht to the hilt until he fell out with him over the issue of rearmament and the planning for war which will be discussed in Chapter 15.

FRANCE

In France the impact of the depression as well as crisis management followed a path which was very different from that followed in Great Britain and Germany. First of all, the impact of the depression was very much delayed in France. The franc was undervalued as it had returned to the gold standard on a very low parity in 1928. France had large gold reserves and was thus in a very comfortable position. It could even go in for the kind of state expenditure mentioned above which was not related to crisis management, but was simply an expression of the fact that France could very well afford such expenditure at that time. Prices of agricultural produce remained high due to protectionism which had been introduced earlier. Industrial production did not recede until 1931. Unemployment was marginal. The repatriation of French capital increased the inflow of gold so that the reserves amounted to much more than the 35 per cent required for the backing of the currency. France was also accused of sterilising gold, but this was not completely true as the inflow of gold was paralleled by a 40 per cent increase in the circulation of banknotes between 1928 and 1931. While the United States, Great Britain and Germany were in the grip of deflation, France enjoyed a stimulating inflationary trend and was yet regarded as a haven of stability to which fugitive foreign capital was attracted.

The British and American devaluations of 1931 and 1933 then cancelled the advantage which France had derived from an undervalued franc and thus the depression entered France in 1934. At the same time the prices of agricultural produce fell due to domestic overproduction caused by protectionism. French capitalists shifted their capital abroad in anticipation of the inevitable devaluation of the franc, but the government hesitated to take this step as it was afraid of ruining the reputation of the country which had so far proved a paragon of stability in an unstable world. An orthodox financial policy was followed in order to support the franc. Deflation, which had so far remained a foreign disease as far as France was concerned, now came upon the French with a vengeance. The Radical Party was the most ardent advocate of an orthodox financial policy at that time and thus showed that 'radical' was a misnomer in this respect. It was only in September 1936 that France arrived at a Tripartite Agreement with the United States and Great Britain which led to a devaluation of the franc by about 30 per cent. For France it would have been much better if such an agreement had emerged from the World Economic Conference, as discussed earlier. But France was not ready for such an agreement in 1933 as it was not willing to make concessions with regard to its tariff policy. If an agreement had been arrived at at that time, it would have saved France a period of reduced industrial production and rising unemployment – though the latter was never such a problem in France as elsewhere. In 1938 French capital was repatriated once more and there was a return to prosperity. But this return of French capital was only achieved after a complicated round of political infighting and frequent changes of government. Rearmament was one issue, the privileges of the working class were another. Rearmament then emerged as a major factor, but it is difficult to assess its role in French recovery. Perhaps the connection was an indirect one: the attack on the privileges of labour in the interest of going ahead with rearmament pleased the capitalists and revived their confidence in the French economy.

SWEDEN

In contrast to the three major European countries discussed so far, Sweden provides a surprising example of how a small country could close its doors to the transmission of the depression by following a wise economic and financial policy. To some extent this was due to good advice by Swedish economists to a government which was prepared to listen to them. But it was also due to the fact that Sweden had no deep home-made crisis to cope with. There had been some trouble with industrial relations and the farmers were disturbed by the fall in prices of their produce, but Sweden's main exposure to the impact of the depression was via its foreign trade.

The Swedish central bank followed a cautious and steady policy aimed at stabilising the price level. It neither indulged in deflationary measures nor did it give in to an inflationary course. Its monetary policy was close to the ideals of the monetarists and they like to cite the Swedish example. Actually Denmark did even better in this respect, but the Swedish economists were more prominent and therefore they got more attention for their subsequent accounts of the Swedish achievements. The performance of the Swedish central bank before September 1931 was quite similar to that of the Bank of England. It tried to stick to the gold standard and was forced to go off it for the same reasons as the Bank of England. Swedish banks had also been in the business of accepting short term deposits and lending money abroad at long term rates. Going off the gold standard was not an automatic reaction to the British decision. The Swedish central bank tried to stick to the gold standard for two more weeks, but the outflow of reserves forced it to follow the British precedent. The bank's period of wisdom began only after that decision. Money supply was tied to a consumer price index which was compiled and published by the bank every week. With regard to the exchange rate the bank actually wanted to follow a course of keeping it down so that Sweden would gain a competitive edge over other countries. But the bank did not have enough reserves to sell Swedish currency abroad, thus driving down the rate. At this juncture it was helped by a financial disaster which came as a great shock to the bank but finally proved to be a boon in disguise.

The disaster was the sudden collapse of the financial empire of Ivar Kreuger who had risen from being the world's largest manufacturer of matches to become one of the world's greatest financial wizards. He shot himself in Paris in March 1932 after he realised that the game was up. The Swedish banks which had given him credit were severely affected and the exchange rate of the Swedish currency dropped, because everybody feared a collapse of the financial system. The Swedish central bank immediately rescued the affected banks and restored confidence in the Swedish system but did nothing to raise the exchange rate, as it had wanted to drive it down anyway. It thus had the best of both worlds: it was admired for its prompt rescue operation and could not be blamed for driving down the exchange rate.

Kreuger's departure from the global financial scene fulfilled one of the conditions which the Swiss banker, Friedrich Somary, had earlier listed as preconditions for a recovery from the depression. The other conditions concerned war debts and reparations and Somary had obviously mentioned Kreuger in this context, because the financial wizard had indulged in a big way in providing private loans to governments, financing them with short term credit which Swedish and American banks gave him very readily. For instance, he had given a loan of $125 million to the German government in 1929 for a period of fifty years. In return he had been granted monopoly rights for the supply of matches to Germany. Kreuger was very creditworthy because of his enormous private wealth, but also because he was perceived to be backed by the solid Swedish banking system. His dramatic fall shows in an exemplary fashion the speculative hallucinations of a world in depression. His death coincided with the most acute stage of the depression in the Western world. The upturn began after he had left this world. Thus Somary's prediction came true. It would be too much to attribute the upturn to this macabre coincidence, but it was a remarkable phenomenon anyhow.

Kreuger's exit also had an immediate consequence for Swedish politics. Prime Minister Ekmann, who had been corrupted by Kreuger, had to resign and this cleared the way for an electoral victory by the social democrats in September 1932. They established a coalition with the association of farmers and remained in control of the government for many years to come. They were able to square the circle as far as the conflicting interests of workers and farmers were concerned. The farmers were looking for higher prices, but that would have affected the real wages of labour. Wages were supposedly too high and the industrialists wanted them to be cut. The government did not cut the wages but increased taxes on wage goods which led to a general rise in prices. Thus the workers were happy, because the government had resisted the demand for a cut in wages and the farmers were happy because agricultural prices were rising. Exporters were happy because the undervalued currency increased their international competitiveness, and those who operated import substituting industries were also happy, because the exchange rate was an instrument of protectionism. It does not come as a surprise that under such conditions the Swedish government had no problem in remaining in office for a long time.

7

TURKEY AND EGYPT
Modernising states at the European periphery

THE ROLE OF THE MODERNISING ELITES

Both Turkey and Egypt had emerged in the early 1920s under 'new management', so to speak. They were ruled by ambitious modernising elites wishing to emulate Europe but also to emancipate themselves from its overbearing tutelage. In Turkey the republican regime of Kemal Pasha, reverently called Ataturk, had rejected the heritage of the Ottoman Empire and established a Turkish nation state which was still in a rather precarious position. The ruling elite preserved its power by means of an authoritarian one-party system. An experiment of permitting the establishment of an opposition party in 1930 was quickly abandoned when this party attracted too much support. Authoritarian rule was not challenged by the majority of the nation which hardly understood the ideas of its modernising elite. At the same time the sovereignty of the new Turkish nation state was severely restricted by its foreign creditors.

In Egypt the nationalist Wafd Party and its popular leader, Zaghlul Pasha, played a role similiar to that of Ataturk and his republicans. But Egypt was a monarchy guided by the British ex-colonial rulers, and its sovereignty was even more impaired than that of Turkey. The social distance between the Egyptian ruling elite and the majority of the people was perhaps even greater than in Turkey. Moreover, due to its cotton export economy Egypt was far more dependent on the world market than was Turkey. The presence of British and French traders was also much more important in Egypt than in Turkey. These foreigners had special privileges and could not be subjected to Egyptian taxation. Thus Egypt was still in a quasi-colonial position and its indigenous elite

74

held a precarious position between the dominant foreigners and a backward peasant population. At the same time the Egyptian state was more closely involved in the management of agriculture than the Turkish one. This activity of the Egyptian state did not necessarily benefit the peasantry but rather the big absentee landowners who controlled large parts of the land devoted to cotton cultivation. Measures to counteract the depression led to an increase in state intervention in both countries. Protective tariffs and price support schemes were introduced so as to help indigenous producers, etc.

The Turkish state took an active interest in industrialisation, but initially there was not much scope for it because no protective tariffs could be introduced in the interests of indigenous industries, as the tariff structure had been dictated by the victorious European powers for the period up to 1929. Turkey had no war debts, but it was still burdened by the old Ottoman debts. The victorious powers had granted a moratorium on the repayment of these debts until 1929. But in the meantime Turkey was under their tutelage in all financial matters. The interest on these debts had to be paid in foreign currency which could only be earned by exporting agrarian produce. The foreign guardians of these debts also acted as the monetary authority for Turkey which could not conduct its own monetary policy before 1929. Just like the Egyptian currency the Turkish one was tied to the British pound. From 1923 to 1929 the exchange rate amounted to 8.15–9.7 lira per pound.

In fact, it was the depression that contributed to a reduction of foreign control as far as both countries were concerned, but its immediate impact meant that they had to jump from the frying pan into the fire. The value of their exports dwindled and they had to curtail their imports drastically. The usual phenomenon of shifting the burden of the depression to the poor people in the countryside could also be witnessed in Turkey and Egypt. The modernising elites were urban ones in both countries and were thus doing comparatively well in the years of the depression. Political leaders did show an interest in the economic problems of the peasantry, as Ataturk did when he toured the countryside in 1931, but they were, of course, primarily interested in the survival of the state and could not afford to be lenient with regard to the taxation of the rural population.

It was an irony of fate that the modernisation of the structure of taxation actually increased the sufferings of the peasantry in the years of the depression. In the Ottoman Empire the state used to claim one tenth of agricultural production as revenue. In practice the state often collected more than that. This was no doubt a retrograde system as it taxed production rather than landed property, but if it had still prevailed during the depression, the state would have shared the peasants' losses caused by the fall in prices. However, in 1925 a modern system of taxation had been introduced in Turkey, based on soil classifications and charges fixed in cash per unit of land. In times of rising prices this was beneficial to the producers, but during the depression it burdened them and contributed to their indebtedness. The Turkish peasants also had to pay taxes on each head of cattle and there was a cess for the construction of roads and railways. In the depression years the government was perplexed when peasants slaughtered their cattle in order to escape taxation and when 10 per cent of the rural population made use of the option of offering their own labour for road construction instead of paying the road cess.

In Turkey the modernising republican government had done away with the old Ottoman tax system, but the British colonial rulers had done this much earlier in Egypt by introducing a land revenue demand quite similar to that prevailing under their rule in Northern India. The demand was fixed in cash at about one third of rental assets. Again this was beneficial to the producers in times of rising prices but proved to be a considerable hardship in the years of the depression. The Egyptian tax collectors were relentless in collecting the revenue, the more so as it had been pledged as a security to the foreign creditors to whom Egypt owed its national debt.

Under the impact of the depression the modernising elites in both countries found it difficult to retain the loyalty of the rural population. Paradoxically it was a saving grace for these elites that their attempts at modernising their nation states had been only partially successful and that the peasantry in the countryside was still isolated, uneducated and helpless and could not organise a joint resistance to their demands. The national elites, in turn, were frustrated by the external pressures which they had to face. These were particularly obvious in terms of the management of the national currencies which was regulated by foreign creditors rather than by the respective national governments.

NATIONAL CURRENCIES, FOREIGN DEBTS AND INTERNATIONAL TRADE

The Turkish lira had a chequered career in the 1920s. It was a paper currency linked to the British pound, but without gold backing. It was officially pegged to the pound and thus to the gold standard only in 1930. There was no central bank in Turkey until 1931. Earlier the Ottoman Bank, which was controlled by Turkey's foreign creditors, was the only bank permitted to issue bank notes. The circulation of these notes was limited as in the interior of the country the old gold and silver coins were still in circulation. The lira provided the link between the domestic economy and the world market. Its exchange rate was subject to seasonal fluctuations. Immediately after the harvest when money was required to buy agricultural produce for export, this demand pushed up the exchange rate. Later on the rate declined and imports for which there was no specific seasonal demand had to be paid for with a seasonally devalued lira. The benefits of devaluation, which have been explained in Chapter 1, did not accrue to Turkey in this way and the terms of trade went against it and particularly against the producers in the countryside. However, from 1926 to 1929 the value of the lira declined not only seasonally but continuously. This was related to a growing deficit in the balance of trade.

The lira' s fall was precipitated in 1929 by a peculiar constellation of events. In 1929 the period during which Turkey's fiscal and monetary policy was under the tutelage of its foreign creditors came to an end, but at the same time the first instalment of the repayment of its foreign debt fell due. Then credit contracted worldwide because of the New York stock market crash of October 1929 and Turkey also had to pay interest on debts incurred for investment in railway construction. Pressed by the foreign creditors the Turkish government embarked on a course of deflation and austerity which, of course, increased the impact of the depression. The budget was balanced with a vengeance, imports were severely curtailed and foreign exchange controls were imposed. Like everybody else in the world, Turkey was then caught unawares by the British departure from the gold standard. But instead of joining the new sterling bloc under British leadership, the Turkish government took the surprising step of linking the lira with the French franc which had remained on the gold standard. This was obviously done in order to preserve the stability of the lira which had just been restored with great efforts in 1930. The authorities concerned believed that this could only be achieved by sticking to the gold standard. Actually the more appropriate step would have been to suspend debt service and devalue the lira in 1931, but obviously the foreign creditors would not have permitted this. Pegging the lira to the franc was to the advantage of these creditors, but it meant an almost unbearable burden for the people of Turkey.

In order to make both ends meet, the Turkish government introduced a regime of very restrictive import quotas, but this, of course, hurt the interests of foreign exporters to Turkey. Thus there arose a bitter conflict of interests between serving foreign debtors and accommodating foreign producers and merchants who were in league with Turkish importers and industrialists depending on foreign investment goods. The responsible Turkish minister had to resign over this and was replaced by Celal Bayar in 1932. Bayar represented the emerging industrial bourgeoisie of Turkey. He advocated state intervention in the interest of the modern capitalist development of the country and he solved the import quota problem by establishing clearing agreements with Turkey's major trading partners. This practically amounted to a kind of barter trade of the coffee-against-machines type which Germany concluded with the Latin American coffee exporting countries (see Chapter 10). Germany, which had already been a major trading partner of Turkey, strengthened its leading position under this new regime. Currencies and exchange rates were more or less irrelevant under this regime, as the agreements were strictly bilateral and were based on the mutually agreed value of the goods exchanged in this way.

At first this new trade regime seemed to be beneficial, but in the long run it subjected Turkey to a new type of dependence. The complementarity of the two economies linked by such a bilateral barter trade was bound to be determined by the stronger partner. Germany was interested in Turkey's raw produce or at most in semi-processed goods. It would see to it that the machines it exported to Turkey would be useful for providing such goods, but would not be interested in fostering industries which could produce substitutes for German machinery.

The position of Egypt was in many ways different from that of Turkey with regard to monetary policy and the conduct of foreign trade though it had the same problem of being under the tutelage of its foreign creditors. The Egyptian pound had been firmly tied to the British pound since 1916. The National Bank of Egypt was no central bank and it was national only in name. It controlled the note issue and practically had the same functions as the Ottoman Bank in Turkey. Fiscal autonomy was granted to Egypt in 1930 and thus it could have its own tariff policy. But clearing agreements were officially prohibited by the British whose prerogatives in this field were terminated only in 1937. Private Egyptian companies did, however, conduct a similar barter trade with foreign companies – particularly with German ones.

The Egyptian system of financial intermediation was far more developed than that of Turkey, mainly due to the role which Egypt played in the world market as a major cotton exporter. Bank Misr, a private bank sponsored by a group of nationalist entrepreneurs, had emerged as the major factor in the cotton trade and also fostered investment in import substituting industries, primarily in textiles and sugar. The scope of government activity with regard to the Egyptian economy was very restricted with the exception of one field – the control of the production of cotton. Since about 80 per cent of Egyptian exports consisted of raw cotton, the government was keen on improving the quality and enhancing the quantity of these exports. This drive also had its problems. An increasing Egyptian population had to be fed and as cotton had replaced grain production, Egypt depended more and more on grain imports. In the years of the depression this did not emerge as a major problem because wheat and cotton prices fell almost to the same extent. The main problem which the government faced in its cotton export policy was rather shortlived. It tried to support the cotton price when the impact of the depression made itself felt but it soon failed in this.

An important type of government intervention was, however, the imposition of a gold export embargo in November 1931. Under the impact of the depression the peasants emptied their hoards and paid their taxes and debts with gold. Between February and July 1931 gold to the value of about one million Egyptian pounds had left the country. This stream of gold increased after Great Britain abandoned the gold standard and the domestic price of gold increased, enhancing the incentives for creditors to press their rural debtors to turn over their hoards to them. In India where the same phenomenon could be witnessed to an even greater extent, the colonial government was not permitted to impose a gold export embargo, but the Egyptian government had the autonomy to introduce such an embargo. The government bought up this distress gold and used it in order to increase the gold reserves backing the Egyptian currency so as to become less dependent on sterling securities, which had so far served that purpose. Until 1936 the government acquired gold worth 7 million Egyptian pounds in this way. It was thus under less pressure to follow a deflationary policy so as to maintain the value of the Egyptian currency. By contrast this was a major problem in India as will be discussed in Chapter 9.

THE FATE OF THE PEASANTRY

In both countries the burden imposed by the depression was shifted to the rural poor. As has been mentioned above, taxation remained at fairly high levels and a retreat into subsistence agriculture was not possible for the peasantry. In Egypt this retreat was physically impossible, because most of the best land was devoted to cotton cultivation. The production of cotton receded only to a very small extent, and the volume of exports was maintained even though their value dwindled. The incidence of agrarian distress is difficult to measure. It can only be gauged by indirect evidence such as the outflow of distress gold in Egypt or the slaughtering of cattle in Turkey, the number of Turkish peasants who turned up for work on road construction as they were unable to pay the road cess, etc. The reduction of the numbers of Egyptian pilgrims to Mecca also throws some light on the condition of the people. While there were 16,000 pilgrims in the years before the depression, there were only 2,262 in 1932 and 1,732 in 1933. School attendance also dropped as peasants could not afford to send their children to school any longer. The per capita consumption of maize and wheat receded in Egypt under the impact of the depression. In the years before the depression it had stood at about 130 kg of maize and nearly 100 kg of wheat; in 1933 these figures had come down to 94 kg and 65 kg respectively, i.e. total per capita consumption of these two food grains had been cut by about 26 per cent. As the cheapness of food benefited the urban classes this reduction must have been concentrated in the countryside whereas urban dwellers probably maintained their previous level of grain consumption.

In Turkey the problems of the rural poor were very similar to those noticed in Egypt. In some regions of Turkey they may have been less pressing than in the cotton dominated Egyptian country-side, because Turkish agricultural export production was smaller and much more diversified (e.g. tobacco, hazel nuts, wine, olives, etc.). On the other hand the much more ambitious Turkish policy of industrialisation and import substitution as well as large scale railway construction schemes combined with an effort at gaining military strength enhanced the burden to be shouldered by the masses of the rural population. Agriculture still had a share of more than 80 per cent of GDP and the absolute value of this share declined from about 800 million lira in the late 1920s to 417 million lira in 1934.

Under conditions of agrarian distress an increase of rural–urban migration could have been expected, but there is little evidence for that in Turkey and Egypt in the 1930s. In Turkey about 20 per cent of the population lived in urban areas. Half of this urban population was concentrated in the few big cities. In Egypt the share of the urban population was even smaller than in Turkey, although population pressure had led to rural–urban migration even before the years of the depression. However, the urban population suffered less under the impact of the depression only because salaries and wages had been fixed in better times and could not be adjusted all of a sudden to the new price level. Thus real wages increased for those who had a job, but unemployed migrants could not hope to benefit from urban life. Thus the rural people remained in the villages and tried to make both ends meet.

8

AUSTRALIA'S REACTION
Overproduction and devaluation

Australia was heavily indebted to British banks on the eve of the depression. It faced a balance of payments crisis and experienced a change of government in October 1929. The Conservatives had to hand over power to the Labour Party which had been in opposition for thirteen years. But the new government had a majority only in the lower house and not in the senate which continued to be dominated by the Conservatives who threw spanners into the works and prevented essential legislation. Moreover, the new government was inexperienced and owed its victory to strikes in mining and industry. The farmers did not figure at all in the Labour Party's political calculations. They were soon pushed into an awful predicament by the government. In order to overcome the balance of payments crisis the government had the bright idea of inaugurating a 'Grow More Wheat' campaign at the most inopportune moment. Wheat export was supposed to earn the foreign exchange which Australia badly needed at that time.

THE 'GROW MORE WHEAT'CAMPAIGN

The Australian farmers who joined this campaign were mostly indebted due to investment in the cultivation of new land in the 1920s. They had cleared 3 million hectares of land for wheat production in this period and now they were supposed to step up production even more. The government encouraged them by making all kinds of promises, e.g. the banks were going to provide credit and the government would guarantee the price of wheat. It turned out later on that the government could not keep these promises because the banks would not provide credit and therefore the legislation for price guarantees was doomed. But the 'Grow More Wheat' campaign did lead to an enormous spurt in wheat production. The farmers followed the government as innocently as the children had followed the pied piper. The land under wheat was expanded by another 1.5 million hectares so as to reach a total of 9 million hectares. This surpassed the combined area under wheat in France, Germany and Great Britain at that time. Plenty of rain contributed to the production of a bumper harvest of about 7.7 million tonnes in 1930. With the worldwide fall in wheat prices the farmers had to face the problem of selling their wheat below the cost of production. The government was hard pressed to rescue them and the Wheat Advances Act was passed in December 1930. But the Commonwealth Bank of Australia was in no mood to foot the bill.

This bank had been established in 1924 and was supposed to act as a central bank for Australia. But except for being responsible for the issue of bank notes it did not really do the work of a central bank, it just did the usual business of a commercial bank and enjoyed a great deal of autonomy. However, it was not headed by experienced bankers but by elder statesmen. The presiding genius was Sir Robert Gibson who had no idea of financial matters. He compensated for that by adopting a very conservative attitude. He did not wish to accommodate the government and he had good reasons for that, because the bank could not tie up its money by giving credit for wheat which could not be sold in the world market. The only alternative for Gibson would have been to advocate a devaluation of the Australian currency. The devaluation did come, but it was not Gibson's idea.

The devaluation of January 1931 helped to export the enormous Australian wheat surplus and thus saved the farmers from bankruptcy. In fact the government even achieved its original aim of solving the balance of payments crisis by exporting wheat. This was, of course, a typical instance of 'exchange dumping', i.e. the export of goods at a price below the cost of production. The internal price remains stable under such conditions while the export price is lowered due to the devaluation. In the long run this would be ruinous for the country concerned and it would also cause the immediate retaliation of other nations (imposition of protective tariffs or of an embargo), but in the short run it can help to overcome a balance of payments crisis, as it did in Australia. Of course, reactions were quick, as we shall see when discussing the

Indian protective tariff on wheat imposed only a few months after the Australian devaluation (see Chapter 9).

THE DEVALUATION OF THE AUSTRALIAN POUND

The Australian devaluation was accomplished in a most unusual manner. Whereas elsewhere governments or central banks would announce a devaluation and peg the currency at a new parity or permit it to float there was no such announcement in the Australian case. The devaluation was allowed to happen because nobody interfered with it. Of course, this was no accident: as we shall see, it was a deliberate sin of omission. This sin could be perpetrated because the Australian pound was pegged to the British pound in such an informal manner that there was no need to change the peg officially as it had never been officially fixed. The Commonwealth Bank of Austria did not bother about exchange rates but left this to the commercial banks which financed external trade by means of the usual short term credits. These banks depended on the large exchange banks abroad which could sell off their holdings of Australian currency in a crisis. This would then automatically lead to a depreciation of the currency. A genuine Australian central bank could have prevented this by buying up Australian pounds, but the Commonwealth Bank did not think that this was its task. It had never experienced a crisis since its foundation in 1924 and therefore it had no reason to think about it. Of course, in the absence of a real central bank the big commercial banks of Australia could have combined in an effort to support the Australian pound, but they usually adjusted their decisions to those of the largest among them, the Bank of New South Wales in Sydney, headed by A.C. Davidson, a very experienced banker. He was the key player in the drama of Australia's sudden devaluation.

Initially Davidson had been convinced that all the Australian banks should act together and raise their interest rates so as to stop the drain of Australia's gold reserves. The other banks did not listen to him at first, but when he raised the interest rate of his bank in January 1930 they followed suit. But soon thereafter Australia faced its balance of payments crisis and the London bankers were afraid that Australia would soon default on its debts. Therefore no

Australian government bonds could be placed in London any longer. The new Labour government then turned to the Australian banks for assistance, but the latter promised to help only if wages were cut and government expenditure radically reduced. This, of course, the Labour government could not do, and there was a complete deadlock.

At this stage the Bank of England intervened and sent its famous trouble shooter, Sir Otto Niemeyer, to Australia. But even before he arrived the Australian banks under Davidson's leadership had arrived at a compromise with the government. Under a 'Mobilisation Agreement' they put a large part of their own sterling assets at the disposal of the government in order to forestall the imposition of exchange controls. By impairing their own reserves in this way, they had to put up with the reaction of foreign banks which paid less for the Australian pound and thus devalued it in practice. Davidson now wanted to act boldly and go in for a radical devaluation of the Australian pound, but he encountered the opposition of Niemeyer who had arrived in Australia in the meantime and was dead set against any devaluation. But the events of the winter 1930–31 justified Davidson's proposal. All Australian banks followed him in his policy of tolerating a devaluation induced by the foreign banks. Finally his bank, the Bank of New South Wales, took the lead in abandoning the old sterling parity in January 1931.

Davidson's critics had predicted that the foreign banks would lower the rate which they paid for Australian pounds and that this would start a downward float which nobody would be able to stop. Concerned about the problems of the Australian wheat and wool exporters, Davidson was obviously prepared to take this risk. The fact that he did nothing to stop the devaluation in the midst of the main exporting season had a double effect of which he was probably very well aware. The depreciation of the Australian pound helped the exporters and at the same time the inflow of export earnings stopped the downward trend of the floating currency. The actual period of floating was very brief, and in the course of it the Australian pound depreciated by about 25 per cent within a few days and then stayed at that level. The British departure from the gold standard in August 1931 blessed the Australian exporters with another devaluation of about 30 per cent. Of course, this was valid only as far as buyers outside the sterling area were concerned.

Australia had entered the depression with hardly any institutional or conceptual equipment which would have enabled it to cope with the crisis in a proper manner: an inexperienced government, no central bank, no official coordination among its commercial banks. Nevertheless, Australia was able to rise to the occasion more quickly than most other countries, and it got along fairly well after the devaluation. India provides a study in contrasts as London did not permit any devaluation of the Indian rupee and also denied India all other means of coping with the depression (see Chapter 9).

9

COLONIAL CRISIS MANAGEMENT
The Indian experience

British India was totally dependent on London as far as its economic policy and its currency were concerned. In London it was not only the Secretary of State for India, but also the treasury and the Bank of England whose views had to be taken into account. All of them insisted that India should be able to pay its tribute punctually and thus retain its creditworthiness. The 'flight from the rupee' was a spectre which haunted them. It was feared that in a panic everybody might wish to sell off government of India bonds and this could lead to a major problem for the British government as it would have to guarantee those bonds. Colonial crisis management was therefore bound to be management in the interest of the creditors and not in the interest of India, which was indebted as a nation and also had among its citizens many indebted peasants and landlords. Deflationary measures carried out on behalf of the creditors increased the burden of debt, while an inflationary policy would have reduced that burden. Even before the depression the government of India had had to follow a deflationary policy in order to maintain the overvalued rupee which had been tied to the gold standard at a rate above the prewar parity. We shall therefore discuss the background of the British Indian currency policy before describing the impact of the depression on India, which was greatly enhanced by the continuation of this deflationary policy.

BRITISH INDIAN CURRENCY POLICY

Until 1893 the Indian currency had been a silver currency. Anybody could bring silver to the mint and get it coined. The seignorage was moderate, as it was supposed to cover the cost of the mint rather than contribute to government revenue. The steady depreciation of silver in the late nineteenth century had a mildly inflationary effect and had shielded India against the fall in agrarian prices (in gold) which had affected almost all other countries of the world. The British were quite happy with this, as the Indian demand for silver helped to support the world price, and London was the centre of the world silver market. But the British authorities were caught on the horns of a dilemma and had to close the mints to the free coinage of silver. This dilemma has been explained in Chapter 2 in the context of the defeat of bimetallism. In 1893 the rupee became a token coin whose exchange rate was managed by the secretary of state for India. For this purpose the secretary of state maintained a gold reserve in London which enabled him to support the rupee in an emergency. The actual instruments of intervention at his disposal were the council drafts and the reverse council drafts. Council drafts were drawn on the government of India, which would provide the buyer with rupees in India. British importers who had to settle bills in India would make use of these drafts, which could be transferred by telegraph. The secretary of state, on the other hand, was spared the trouble of remitting money from India to London for the payment of the 'home charges'. By providing liquidity to the finance of trade in this way the secretary of state could manage the exchange rate of the rupee within a rather narrow band. In a way his releasing or witholding of council drafts could be compared to the open market policies of central banks. If in spite of this careful management of the currency there was a sudden depreciation of the rupee, he could sell reverse council drafts, i.e. buy rupees. This would dimish his reserves in London and thus it had some limits, though in an emergency the secretary of state could have borrowed money easily in London in order to buy more rupees. In fact, he was only called upon very rarely to issue reverse council drafts. The exchange rate of 1 rupee to 1s 4d was maintained by the secretary of state for a long time and it was therefore considered to be a kind of 'natural' rate. Actually it was determined in a completely arbitrary manner by the secretary of state; it was not fixed by any law or government resolution until 1927 when the Currency Act of that year fixed the rate at 1s 6d.

The silver standard abandoned in 1893 with the closure of the Indian mints to the free minting of that metal was replaced by a gold exchange standard which was praised by Keynes in his first book which was devoted to Indian currency and finance. This standard had the advantage of providing the currency with a gold backing but avoiding the circulation of gold coins which would have made additional demands on the limited gold resources of the world. In enjoying a gold backing but circulating silver coins India seemed to have the most practical currency regime imaginable. As long as silver was cheap and the secretary of state could manage the currency in the manner described above, this was an ideal arrangement. But when the silver price increased and the silver content of the token coin circulating in India exceeded its nominal value, the secretary of state had a problem. In order to prevent the people from melting down their rupees, he would have to adjust the exchange rate upward. This happened in the First World War. In the immediate postwar years the price of silver fell once more. But now a downward adjustment of the exchange rate could have led to a flight from the rupee, so the secretary of state tried to support the exchange rate by buying rupees, i.e. issuing reverse council drafts. He exhausted his reserves in this way and greatly incensed the Indian public as this policy was so obviously not in the interest of India but only of its creditors.

When the secretary of state was at the end of his tether he could only revert to a slower but more effective policy of deflation. The minting of silver coins was stopped in 1922 and old coins returned to the government were melted down. This also provided some additional income to the government which could much more easily balance its budget in this way. From 1922–27 the government of India melted down coins worth 400 million rupees and thus reduced the silver currency in circulation from 3.5 to 3.1 billion rupees. It could have compensated for that by increasing the circulation of paper currency, but it increased the notes in circulation only from 1.5 to 1.6 billion rupees. Due to this deflationary policy the exchange rate of the rupee rose to 1s 6d in 1927 and was then fixed at that rate by legislation. The government argued that this was the current market rate of the rupee and that nothing had been done to manipulate it. But critics could point to the long term deflationary policy followed since 1922, when attacking this rate, which was after all 12.5 per cent above the prewar level of 1s 4d. This issue became a very contentious one and greatly contributed to the rise of economic nationalism among Indian businessmen. The overvalued rupee provided a bonus to importers and thus harmed the import substituting Indian textile industry. It also impeded Indian exports, which was a problem for the British as India always had to have an export surplus so as to pay for the 'home charges'. In this respect the creditors were on the horns of a dilemma. If the rupee remained overvalued there was no danger of a 'flight from the rupee', but if this endangered the export surplus, India's debt service could be affected and thus the spectre of the 'flight from the rupee' would raise its ugly head in another corner of the precarious edifice of British Indian finance.

Being stuck with the new rate of 1s 6d the British could only defend it by means of further deflation. From 1927–31 the silver coins in circulation were reduced from 3.1 to 2.2 billion rupees and the note circulation was reduced from 1.6 to 1.5 billion rupees. This amounted to a contraction of money supply by 21 per cent. The finance member of the government of India, Sir George Schuster, who had to execute this policy, was convinced that it was wrong, but he had to obey his masters in London. When Great Britain abandoned the gold standard in September 1931, Schuster tried to uncouple the rupee from the pound. If the pound was free to float, why should the rupee not be permitted to float, too? His masters in London immediately revoked this measure and forced him to maintain the old exchange rate. This meant that he was compelled to continue the deflationary policy which greatly magnified the impact of the depression. Schuster's successors had to follow this policy throughout the 1930s. There was a slight reprieve in 1935–36 but in 1937 the deflationary measures were stepped up once more. The currency in circulation was thus reduced by 40 per cent between 1922 and 1938. The official excuse for this policy was that the government had to reduce money supply in keeping with the reduction of economic activity. This was a case of 'perverse flexibility' (Currie, 1934) but, of course, the government knew what it was doing and only used this excuse in order to confuse its critics. The deflationary policy was continued even at a time when most other governments had long since started to reflate their economies.

This policy put an enormous pressure on all debtors in India. The income of the peasants had been cut by half due to the fall in agricultural prices, but their debts were enhanced by the deflationary policy. This has been explained earlier by referring to the debt–deflation theory of Irving Fisher (see p. 11). Therefore the peasants had to sell their wives' gold ornaments or sell some of their land to richer neighbours and money lenders. When Great Britain left the gold standard in 1931, the price of gold increased by 30 per cent and the money lenders put pressure on their clients to hand over their gold to them, otherwise they would have to foreclose their mortgages. The enormous stream of 'distress gold' which flowed out of India in this way helped to support the sterling bloc. The British had not expected this flood, and Schuster was amazed when he saw the piles of beautiful gold ornaments in the government of India's currency office. But once the stream of gold was there, the British did everything to perpetuate it. The officers of the government of India used to state in public that this stream was simply due to the fact that the Indians sold their gold because they got a good price for it, but in secret files they admitted that deflation and indebtedness made the peasants part with their gold. The stream of gold which provided India with a comfortable export surplus throughout the years of the depression solved all the problems the British had faced before. The overvalued rupee was supported by this flow of gold and there was no problem about remitting the 'home charges'. The spectre of the 'flight from the rupee' was laid to rest and did not raise its head again. The edifice of British Indian finance now had a solid foundation, built on the distress of India's indebted peasants. By 1932 India had parted with gold worth 3 billion rupees, while Great Britain now held gold reserves worth £825 million (11 billion rupees). In September 1931 when Great Britain left the gold standard British gold reserves had amounted to £130 million (c. 1.7 billion rupees).

THE FALL OF PRICES IN INDIA

When the wheat price declined in the world market, the Indian wheat price had to adjust to it immediately. India hardly exported any wheat at that time and supply and demand in the home market remained stable. But cheap Australian wheat could be imported and the Indian price level could not be shielded against it. The imposition of a protective tariff was only conceived at a later stage, as we shall see. The price of millet and other coarse cereals immediately followed the wheat price as wheat could have been substituted for them in the consumer market, though not in terms

91

of production as wheat would not grow where these coarse cereals were cultivated in the high lands of India. The rice of Eastern India was at first not affected by this price fall, as we have seen when discussing world rice production. The people of Eastern India were not used to wheat and did not even have the implements for preparing food made from it. The fall of the rice price was brought about by external forces and not by the substitution of wheat for rice by Indian consumers.

Peasant unrest had spread in India in the second half of 1930, but it was initially restricted to the wheat areas. In the beginning of 1931 the government of India was faced with the prospect of large scale unrest, because by then the rice price had come down, too, and Australian 'exchange dumping' of wheat threatened to depress the Indian price of wheat even further. Moreover, the main wheat growing area was the Punjab which was the home of most soldiers of the British Indian army. This was an additional reason for protecting the wheat growers, and therefore a protective tariff on wheat was imposed in the summer of 1931 before that year's harvest would come to the market. The Indian wheat price recovered promptly and even surpassed the rice price in 1933, a totally unprecedented event, because rice had always been more expensive than wheat. This abnormal situation did not prevail for long. The wheat price fell again, but this time due to indigenous overproduction induced by the protective tariff. Bad harvests then pushed up the price levels of both rice and wheat. After 1934 the prices developed along parallel lines with the rice being once more about 30 per cent dearer than wheat.

The rice growers also clamoured for a protective tariff, but the government of India did not want to listen to them. There was a simple reason for this: India, which still included Burma, was a rice exporting country. There was even a rice export tax which provided a good revenue to the government. It was inconceivable to impose both a protective tariff on imports and a tax on exports. But those who asked for the protective tariff also had good reasons for their demand. There was a brisk trade in the world market in broken rice, which earlier had been used only as raw material for industrial starch. The impoverished peasants of India now ate this imported broken rice, which reduced the demand for rice in the Indian home market. After long negotiations a protective tariff was imposed on the import of broken rice in 1935.

PURCHASING POWER AND IMPORT
SUBSTITUTION

The deflationary policy which depressed the price level in India also reduced the purchasing power of the masses. This also reduced the attraction of India as a market for British goods. The middle class, which lived on fixed salaries and thus benefited from low prices, was still too small to provide a really substantial market for imported goods. The Indian cotton textile industry which registered some growth during the years of the depression was fighting on two fronts. On the one hand it was faced with foreign competition, particularly with regard to Japanese products, while on the other it had to compete with the handloom weavers. Whereas the industry could not reduce its wages immediately, the handloom weavers had cheap food and cheap cotton and could therefore operate very economically. In fact, these weavers were the pioneers of import substitution and the textile industry followed them, conquering step by step the market which the handloom weavers had reclaimed in the first place.

As far as Japanese competition was concerned, the British helped the Indian industry by imposing protective tariffs combined with 'imperial preference', i.e. preferential tariffs for British goods. This amounted to a kind of market sharing between British and Indian producers who were both interested in keeping third parties out. No similar arrangement could be made to fight the competition of the handloom weavers. Moreover, the Indian industrialists kept their mouths shut in this respect, because the handloom weavers were in the good books of Gandhi and the Indian National Congress.

The growth of Indian textile production in the years of the depression was only due to population growth. Per capita demand for textiles stagnated or even receded. At the end of the 1930s it became obvious that the Indian textile industry was facing an insurmountable barrier as import substitution had reached its limits due to the reduced purchasing power of the Indian masses. The war came at just the right time. Procurement of textiles for the British army solved the problems of the Indian textile industry.

The only import substituting industry which registered a phenomenal success in the depression years was the sugar industry. It was shielded against foreign competition by a prohibitive tariff directed against the import of refined sugar from Java.

Since no British imperial interests were at stake in this case, the government of India was not averse to imposing such a tariff once it had given up its earlier free trade principles. Sugar mills proliferated at a rapid pace and the production of sugar cane expanded. India was soon self-sufficient with regard to refined sugar. The increasing consumption of tea in the Indian home market at that time may also have helped in raising the demand for refined sugar, but by 1937 the sugar industry faced a barrier which can be compared to that of the textile industry. The poor masses consumed unrefined village sugar and the Indian market was saturated with refined sugar. Export was the only chance for further growth, but sugar was overproduced in the world market and the International Sugar Agreement of 1937 divided the world into sugar exporting and importing countries. The exporting countries got export quotas, the importing countries – by defini-tion – were not entitled to them. India was classified as an importing country. This time imperial interests were at stake and the secretary of state for India was told in no uncertain terms by his cabinet colleague responsible for the colonies that there could be no sugar quota for India. This was a severe blow for the Indian sugar industry which then tried hard to maintain the internal price level by means of cartels and a restriction of production.

THE EXPORT INDUSTRIES: JUTE AND TEA

The export industries were mostly based in Eastern India, and were not in Indian but in British hands, or, to be more precise, in Scottish hands. Raw jute was grown by small peasants in their rice fields. If the demand for jute receded, they could turn back to rice cultivation. The steep decline of the rice price precluded this alternative in the depression years. Raw jute was thus very cheap and the jute mill owners could compensate their losses by shifting the burden to the jute growing peasants. The mill owners were organised in the Indian Jute Mills Association (IJMA) which tried to restrict its members' production so as to maintain the prices for jute cloth and gunny bags. This kind of policy faced two obstacles: for one thing, there were 'outsiders', mostly Indian jute mill owners, who did not abide by the discipline imposed by the IJMA; and, for another, the members of the IJMA often paid only lip service to this discipline and secretly produced more than they were supposed to. Tariffs, of course, could not help this export industry: at the most, the government could have helped enforce internal discipline. The IJMA appealed to the government, but to no avail, and at a later stage its members were equally keen to reject government intervention.

The tea industry was in a much better position in this respect. The few big companies which owned tea plantations as well as tea factories and shipping agencies and also kept in touch with their competitors abroad could enforce discipline through their Tea Association in a far more effective way than the IJMA could ever hope to do. They saw to it that an international agreement was arrived at which included the Netherlands Indies (Indonesia) and Ceylon (Sri Lanka), then turned around and compelled the government of India to enforce this agreement. At first a notification was issued under the Sea Customs Act and then a Tea Protection Act was passed in 1933. The agents of the Tea Association were given access to the British Indian customs offices where they physically controlled the strict observance of the export quotas. The average price for a pound of tea had amounted to 0.66 rupees in 1930, but had declined to 0.57 rupees in 1931 and 0.45 in 1932. By 1933, after the controls has been imposed, the price rose once more to 0.62. It steadily increased in subsequent years and reached 0.73 rupees in 1937. The strict controls had done the trick, but the prediction of a sceptical British officer came true that such controls, if once imposed, would not easily be lifted later on. Initially the tea control act was valid only for five years, but it was promptly renewed in 1938.

THE POLITICAL CONSEQUENCES OF COLONIAL CRISIS MANAGEMENT

The crisis hit the Indian peasants who did not get any help from the government, except for those in the Punjab who were blessed with a protective tariff on wheat. The deflationary policy of the British was criticised by all Indian interest groups. Many who would otherwise have had reasons to disagree found a common denominator in opposition to this British policy. The National Congress could thus attain a much broader social base for the freedom movement. Gandhi's Salt March in the spring of 1930 was initially not at all connected with the impact of the depression, but the campaign dovetailed with peasant unrest which became acute after the wheat harvest reached the market in July 1930. The British unwittingly drove the peasants into the arms of the Congress. But the peasants were vulnerable and could go along with a nationalist campaign only to a certain extent. Their land could be confiscated if they refused to pay land revenue. In 1932 the government of India started a draconian campaign of repression which cowed the peasants. This would have continued to work if the government had been able to rule with an iron fist for ever, but constitutional reforms were in the offing and the government hoped that the peasants would vote for pro-British parties rather than for the Congress. However, depression and repression ruined these political calculations.

This course of events turned the Congress into a peasants'party, but it was also supported by the industrialists who saw that an investment in nationalism was their best bet. Left-wing national-ists like Jawaharlal Nehru and his followers did not quite trust the industrialists and feared a 'fascist compact' between British and Indian businessmen. The attempts at market sharing mentioned earlier seemed to point in this direction, but the shortsighted policy of the colonial rulers in the interest of British creditors did not permit such a 'fascist compact'. Colonial crisis management paved the way for decolonisation in several ways: reduced purchasing power impaired India's attractiveness as a market for British goods, and widespread unrest made colonial rule more precarious and expensive. On the other hand, it strengthened the National Congress and thus helped to build an organisation to which power could be transferred in the end. This was, of course, an unintended by-product of British policy.

There was another factor which hastened the advent of decolonisation. The depression had lowered the prices of raw produce all over the world and the control of colonies became less attractive, particularly when the cost of administration increased whereas revenue income diminished. The British Indian land revenue system practically collapsed in the years of the depression and customs duties also declined with the contraction of trade. The only reason for holding on to colonial rule was the problem of the national debt which India owed to British creditors. When Jawaharlal Nehru visited his Labour Party friends in England in 1938, this problem was a subject of discussion. How could the Labour Party advocate Indian independence if this question was not settled beforehand? The party was by no means an ardent advocate of Indian independence except for a few 'Friends of

India', and when Labour came to power in 1945 it had no contingency plan on what to do with India. But at least it did not have to worry about the Indian debt any longer. The war had solved this problem, because at the end of it Great Britain was indebted to India, whose debt had been wiped out by the production of Indian industry in the service of the British war effort. Since Great Britain had procured everything on credit in India, there was even a large balance in India's favour with the Bank of England. It proved to be much easier to grant independence to a creditor than to a debtor.

There is no doubt that decolonisation owed much to this turn of events. But there was another element which has to be taken into account. About two million Indian soldiers had served in the British Indian army during the war, they had seen a great deal of the world and they knew how to handle modern arms. The majority of them had to be demobilised after the war and most of them belonged to peasant families. As long as they had been in service they had remained loyal to the British, but could they be expected to remain loyal if they were no longer in service and might be subjected to repression once the colonial rulers were challenged by another campaign by the freedom movement? The memories of the 1930s were still fresh. During the war a kind of military law had prevailed, but this could not be continued in times of peace. Discretion is the better part of valour – and so was decolonisation.

10

THE NEW ROLE OF THE
STATE IN LATIN AMERICA

All Latin American states were economically very vulnerable, as the impact of the depression showed in a most dramatic way. They exported either agricultural produce or minerals and ores whose prices were falling even before the depression, and after 1929 they declined very rapidly. Exports receded and therefore imports had to be curtailed severely. Debt service and the flight of capital reduced the means available for imports even more. There were two 'buffers' which shielded the states of Latin American to some extent. First, many imports were non-essential and could be omitted easily, and second, large numbers of unemployed workers and agricultural labourers would go back to the countryside and simply fade away. The fate of those people has hardly been studied and they tend to be forgotten in the relevant literature. Presumably they returned to subsistence agriculture, but as pointed out earlier, subsistence agriculture may be a myth which hides suffering behind a smokescreen of bucolic charm. Nevertheless, both buffers enabled indigenous businessmen to accumulate capital and to invest in the home market, thus overcoming the effects of the depression. The first buffer stimulated import substitution, the second one helped to keep wages low and to shift the burden of the depression to the rural poor. The deteriorating terms of trade of the periphery were paralleled by a similar shift of the terms of trade to the disadvantage of the rural people.

Latin American economists have highlighted the importance of the depression as a turning point in the economic development of Latin America. By uncoupling themselves from the world market and concentrating on the home market, the Latin Americans had reduced their dependence on foreign countries and cultivated some inner strength. Import substitution is stressed heavily in this respect while the conditions of the rural poor are conveniently forgotten. There is no doubt that the governments of many Latin American states felt compelled to foster self-reliance and to adopt measures in favour of indigenous industries, etc. Some progress was made in this direction, but it was also accompanied by an increase in state interventionism and a general distrust of the old ideas of free trade. The enthusiasm for import substitution and internal development of the economists associated with the Economic Commission for Latin America has influenced the interpretation of the economic history of the 1930s to such an extent that a more sober historical analysis tends to be neglected. These economists, so to speak, magnified the roots of import substitution in the 1930s as they looked back at them from the position of a subsequent period when import substitution had definitely made a mark. But the recovery from the depression was to a much larger extent due to the revival of exports than these economists tended to believe. However, even though import substitution may have to be given a lesser weight when assessing the economic history of Latin America in the 1930s, the emergence of state intervention was certainly a dominant feature of this period. It also played a role in export promotion by means of multiple exchange rates or bilateral trade agreements. The diversification of agricultural production was another sphere of active state intervention. Agricultural import substitution was in some states perhaps as important as industrial import substitution.

'REACTIVE' AND 'PASSIVE' STATES

Not all Latin American states were equally active in the field of interventionism. C. F. Díaz Alejandro has therefore distinguished between 'reactive' and 'passive' states: the first ones used a whole panoply of interventionist measures, the others just waited for an improvement of conditions in the world market. Such passive states were quasi-colonies like Cuba or 'banana republics' like Honduras whose sovereignty was very much restricted. But even among the reactive states there were many differences with regard to the instruments used. Some of them devalued their currencies, imposed customs duties, stepped up state expenditure and tried to reflate the economy (e.g. Brazil and Columbia). Others were satisfied with only one measure, like Peru, which devaluated its currency and then waited for a recovery of the export market. The type of reaction was conditioned by the respective country's previous history, by the export commodities it had to offer and by the availability of the instruments of intervention. In countries whose export sector was limited to certain enclaves dominated by foreign companies which had to weather the storm of the depression by themselves, there was hardly any scope for state intervention. This was the case with Peru, which mostly exported oil and ores. The coffee-exporting countries like Brazil and Columbia were faced with an altogether different situation as the production of these commodities was in indigenous hands. Finally, Argentina, which exported grain and beef and competed with European and North American producers in this respect was in a category by itself, and could not be compared to any of the other Latin American countries.

In reviewing the reactions of the different Latin American states we shall start with the 'super-reactive' ones, the coffee-exporters Brazil and Columbia. They were obliged to protect the interests of the indigenous coffee planters who were also potential investors in the home market, whereas states whose exporters were mostly foreigners, as in Peru, could hardly hope that these people would be interested in investing in import substitution and thus help to develop the home market. Therefore interventionism did not make much sense in such cases and the governments stuck to the old ideology of free trade. Moreover, the states which depended on foreign exporters were used to deriving their revenue from moderate export taxes, they hardly taxed their own people, and therefore had no information and no instruments of state intervention. In this respect Brazil and Columbia were very different from most other Latin American countries.

BRAZIL AND COLUMBIA

Brazil had introduced a certain amount of state intervention even before the depression. This was aimed at stabilising the coffee price by means of the state-supported procurement of surplus coffee. It was managed by a special bank which gained a great deal of influence over the economic fate of the nation. In addition, Brazil as a sovereign state could, of course, control its own currency and monetary policy though it had to respect the views of foreign creditors to some extent. The early 1920s had been a period of easy money, followed by a deflationary policy in 1923. By that time

Brazil already had a textile industry of its own and there were other industries as well. The textile industry had made a good deal of profit in the early 1920s. The appreciation of the currency in the deflationary period (1923–26) had both a positive and a negative impact on this industry: positive to the extent that imported textile machinery was cheaper, and negative because of the increase of competition from foreign textiles. Initially the positive effect made itself felt, investment increased and textile machines were imported, but this led to the creation of overcapacities and to keen competition in the home market. In combination with the negative effect mentioned above, this led to a steep fall in textile prices. Subsequently there was once more a period of easy money and of a depreciating exchange rate which gave a reprieve to the textile industry. But it was only due to the devaluation at the time of the depression that the textile industry could recover and fully utilise the capacities which had been installed earlier. Other industries also benefited from this development. The index of industrial production (1928=100) receded to 91 in 1930, but it subsequently rose very steadily and reached 160 in 1936.

In spite of this industrial success story coffee production remained by far the most important sector of the Brazilian economy. The volume of exports remained more or less the same, but their value had declined by 50 per cent. The government at first continued its policy of buying up surplus coffee so as to support the export price, but this scheme collapsed in 1931. Storage room was no longer available and thus surplus coffee was simply burned. The radical devaluation then improved the chances of the coffee exporters once more. At the same time the government propagated the cultivation of cotton so as to diversify agricultural production.

In 1934 Brazil concluded a bilateral trade agreement with Germany which can be summed up by the formula 'coffee for machines'. This was a new kind of international barter trade which circumvented the shrinking of world trade due to the contraction of credit and the imposition of exchange controls. In this context it was very important for Brazil that the United States, its largest trading partner and creditor, would tolerate such new arrangements. The attitude of the United States differed in this respect from that adopted by the British in their relations with Argentina. Of course, there were also dissident voices in the United States recommending the imposition of an import duty on Brazilian coffee so as to bring the recalcitrant debtor to heel. But Cordell Hull, secretary of state in the Roosevelt administration, pursued an internationalist policy and nothing was done to obstruct Brazilian trade policies. Hull was interested in enhancing the political stature of Brazil as a leading power in Latin America, the more so as the United States had been caught on the wrong foot in 1930 when it had supported the opposition to Vargas.

The coup led by Getulio Vargas in 1930 had been no social revolution but simply the replacement of one kind of political elite by another. The losers were the 'liberal' coffee planters of Sao Paulo who had up to then controlled Brazilian politics. Vargas had been the governor of Rio Grande do Sul, a border province with a social and economic profile quite different from that of the central coffee region. Small landholders and cattle breeders predominated in Rio Grande. They produced mostly for the Brazilian home market and had to compete with Brazil's southern neighbours. The provincial government had a tradition of interventionism and active modernisation informed by the positivism of Auguste Comte. Vargas represented that tradition and emerged as a strong contender for the presidency in the elections of 1930, which he lost. His supporters were not confined to his home province, for the political alternative which he projected was also attractive to army officers who were inspired by revolutionary nationalism. With their help Vargas was able to stage a successful coup. The impact of the depression served as a catalyst in bringing about this political constellation.

Vargas was a clever manipulator rather than a revolutionary firebrand. He acted as an umpire balancing various interests, showing his hand only when his power was directly challenged. At first he continued the subsidies to the coffee planters, but at the same time he had to assert national control over banking and exchange rate policies and this alienated the 'liberals' of Sao Paulo. They had resented the loss of political power and now they were even more incensed by being overruled in the financial and economic sphere. Thus in 1932 they rose in rebellion. Vargas suppressed this rebellion and had remained *persona non grata* in Sao Paulo ever since. In 1934 he introduced a new constitution, and was then elected president by indirect election. In 1935 a communist-inspired popular front did him the favour of opening a direct attack on him. He crushed it and got a great deal of political mileage out of magnifying the communist danger. In his anti-communist crusade he was supported by a proto-fascist movement, the so called 'integralists', who attracted sympathies among army officers and the middle classes. Their ideology was rural and retrograde. They stressed Brazilian nationalism and the need for strengthening the Catholic church. Their programme had a vague social appeal, and some sections of the church supported them for all these reasons.

Vargas feigned sympathy with the 'integralists' until 1937 when he staged another coup and eliminated them, too. Having established his authoritarian control over the country, he could proceed with his modernising interventionism which he had imbibed in his earlier years in Rio Grande. In this he was ably assisted by Oswaldo Aranha, an old friend from Rio Grande, who served as his chief political planner and administrative reformer in his first cabinet, and was then instrumental in forging links with the USA as ambassador in Washington. He had been sent there initially in 1934 in order to get him out of the country, where he did not quite fit into the system. He was also averse to the new turn of events in 1937 when Vargas established his 'Estado Novo'. Nevertheless, he joined the new cabinet as foreign minister in 1938. As a convinced anti-fascist Aranha favoured an alliance with the United States whereas Vargas wanted to hold the balance between pro-German and pro-American pressure groups in Brazil. The issue was finally settled by the outbreak of the war, when Aranha's policy prevailed.

Brazil was able to use all the instruments available for crisis management in the depression. The convertibility of the Brazilian currency was effectively suspended at the end of 1929, but the gold standard had not yet been abandoned – this happened only at the end of 1930. Brazil also suspended international debt service, imposed controls on foreign exchange, adopted a reflationary monetary policy, supported the import-substituting indigenous industry and diversified its main export products. Not all of these measures were equally successful, but in general Vargas could be fully satisfied with his crisis management. The other side of the coin was, of course, that the poor had to adjust to the harsh conditions imposed upon them by the depression. No attempt was made to help them by means of state intervention. The emerging bourgeois state led by Vargas did not aspire to becoming a welfare state.

Crisis management in Columbia was to some extent similar to

that of Brazil, but there were also some interesting differences. In both countries coffee accounted for 70 per cent of exports and both countries had an incipient industry capable of going in for more import substitution. But in contrast with Brazil, Columbia also had oil, in which the American oil companies were very much interested. However, the oil economy remained an enclave which had no important influence on the Columbian economy in general. In the 1920s Columbia had a windfall of $20 million, as it was compensated for the loss of Panama which the Americans had snatched away from it, so as to be able to control the Panama Canal. Without the interest of the American oil companies in Columbian oil, the US government would hardly have agreed to pay such generous compensation. The inflow of this money, which started in 1921, led to the 'Dance of the Millions' in Columbia. A good deal of this money was spent on importing consumer goods, but nevertheless investment goods had a share of 30 per cent of total imports. This helped the import-substituting industries such as the textile industry, etc. The potential for further progress along those lines was great and the impact of the depression fell on fertile ground in this respect.

The shock of the depression led to a changing of guards in Columbia. The conservative planters, the 'Cafeteros', lost power to liberal politicians representing the emerging bourgeoisie. President Olaya (1930–34) immediately followed Great Britain in leaving the gold standard, devalued the Columbian peso against the US dollar by 70 per cent, and introduced tough foreign exchange controls and a protectionist policy. The devaluation led to a steep increase in real wages in 1932, but this benefited only those workers who had not been fired when the country was hit by the depression. The masses of the unemployed returned to the countryside and clashed with the 'Cafeteros' who did not want to accommodate them. But the government was able to overcome this unrest. In 1934 President Olaya, who could be called liberal-conservative, was replaced by a liberal-socialist successor whose policies will be discussed in Chapter 14, which is devoted to the political consequences of the depression. The new constitution which he introduced in 1936 was a remarkable document due to its emphasis on social justice. It proved to be very difficult to achieve the goals set by that constitution, but it was nevertheless important that an attempt was made to raise political consciousness in this way.

104

Columbia's main export, both before and after the depression, was coffee. In this it shared the same fate as Brazil. One might have expected that the two countries would have got together and adopted a common policy of output and export restrictions as India, Ceylon and the Netherlands Indies had done with regard to tea, but this did not happen. The Columbian coffee producers preferred to let the Brazilians go ahead and burn their coffee so as to improve the chances for Columbian coffee exports. They had adopted the same attitude with regard to the Brazilian price stabilisation policy in earlier years and thus enjoyed a free ride. Moreover, Columbian coffee was of a better quality and therefore always had an edge over Brazilian coffee in the world market. Columbia also benefited from a bilateral trade agreement with Germany of the 'coffee for machines' type. It thus experienced an upswing from 1934 onwards and could afford substantial investments in its industry.

CHILE AND PERU

In contrast with the coffee exporters, Chile and Peru mostly exported ore, and Peru also exported oil. They were both hit very hard by the depression. Chile was even rated in statistical terms as the country most affected by the depression in the whole world. International trade in general receded only by 25 per cent during the depression years, but Chile's exports were reduced by 76 per cent and its imports by 82 per cent. Peru was similarly affected, but on taking a second look we see that the two countries were not hit so terribly hard by the depression as the figures concerning their external trade would indicate. The reasons for this were not the same in Chile as in Peru. Chile had a substantial industry even before the depression, and this industry experienced only a slight recession and otherwise continued to grow throughout the depression years. Peru was underdeveloped when compared to Chile, but since its export sector was dominated by foreign companies, their losses, caused by the depression, had little direct effect on Peru. Nevertheless Peru experienced a major political crisis.

Chile had departed from the gold standard in June 1931, and had asked its foreign creditors for a moratorium on its debts. The Chilean peso depreciated in the course of these events, and the deflationary policy maintained until June 1931 was given up. It

105

was followed by a reflationary policy which soon became an inflationary one. Within two years money supply (M1) doubled. A shortlived socialist government, which was in office only from June to September 1932, explicity ordered the central bank to print money so as to revive the economy. This met with some success, but not for the socialist government, whose days were numbered. The index of industrial production (1929=100) fell to 76 in 1931 and then rose again to 123 in 1937. Chile also profited from a reviving demand for copper and other ores which it exported. Ore output had dwindled rapidly before 1932 but almost regained its pre-depression level in 1937.

Peru experienced a similar recovery, but this was due to somewhat different reasons. In the 1920s Peru had undergone a fundamental structural change of the composition of its exports. In earlier years cotton, copper and silver had been predominant, but in the 1920s oil had become of foremost importance. In this period Peru was ruled by President Leguia who was in the pay of the foreign oil companies and ran the country so as to suit their interests. He secured his regime by corruption, but the depression deprived him of the means for continuing this game and he was overthrown in August 1930. This was followed by a civil war which lasted for three years. No crisis management was possible at that time. Peru benefited only from the fact that it had declared its insolvency and devalued its currency at the first impact of the depression. When the civil war was over, prices for the export products recovered. In the meantime Peru had also revived its cotton exports which had amounted to one third of all exports as late as 1925. The immediate impact of the depression had also curtailed the cotton export (1928=100, 1931=61), but by 1934 the index reached 168 – a phenomenal revival for this type of export.

ARGENTINA AND MEXICO

These two countries deviate in many respects from the pattern set by the countries discussed so far. Argentina's main exports, beef and wheat, its enormous war profit during the First World War and its special relationship with Great Britain were all without parallel in Latin America. Mexico, on the other hand, was unique due to its early revolution after the overthrow of the dictator, Porfirio Díaz, in 1911 and the constant tensions, as well as the intimate contacts with the United States.

Argentina was almost complementary in its agricultural production to Great Britain which had concentrated on industrial production and had greatly reduced its internal output of grain. British wheat production had receded from an average of 2 million tonnes during the First World War to 1 million tonnes in 1931. The number of British cattle amounted to about 7 million, which was only half that of France. Therefore the British were good customers of the Argentinian grain producers and cattle breeders. On the other hand Argentina was a much appreciated client of the British capital market. For this reason Argentina tried to remain in the good books of its British creditors and did not suspend debt service, although it did introduce foreign exchange controls and allowed its currency to depreciate. Argentina was by far the richest country in Latin America and had a large amount of gold reserves. Nevertheless, it suspended the convertibility of its currency as early as December 1929, which amounted to abandoning the gold standard in practice. In the years 1927 to 1929 the value of Argentinian exports had always amounted to about $1 billion, and the imports were also substantial, but there had been a positive balance of trade to the tune of $150 to $200 million in those years. These external trade figures were about twice as high as those of Brazil and four times higher than those of Mexico. The value of Argentina's exports fell less than that of the coffee exporting countries in the depression years and its imports also remained fairly high. There was only once a negative balance of trade, of about $100 million, in 1930. In the years from 1932 to 1934 Argentinian exports were worth about $370 million, and the positive balance of trade amounted to about $125 million.

In spite of enjoying such a comfortable position, Argentina concluded a bilateral trade agreement with Great Britain in 1933 which was not at all favourable for the Argentinians. Great Britain exploited its position as a creditor and included preferential tariffs for British industrial products in this agreement. As a compensation, Argentinian beef was granted free access to the British market. The British could hardly have bought their beef more cheaply elsewhere, so this concession was a sham. But the Argentinian cattle breeders were so interested in this guarantee that they did not care for the consumers and industrialists who were affected by the preferential treatment accorded to British products in this agreement. The United States protested in vain, and Keynes showed his mercantilist colours by defending this bilateral agreement. He argued that a British worker who ate Argentinian beef could well expect that his job would be secured by the export of British industrial products to Argentina. It is understandable that import substitution did not have much of a chance in Argentina under such conditions although this rich country would have had the means to sponsor industrial growth by investing in production for the home market.

Mexico was very poor compared to Argentina. Like Peru it depended on foreign companies for its oil and ore exports. Unlike other Latin American countries Mexico had a great deal of experience in state intervention. But as far as monetary policy was concerned it followed a very orthodox line even in the midst of the depression. It initially did not even make use of the fact that it had a bimetallic currency, as it produced silver and had silver coins in circulation. The exchange rate was determined by the relation of the silver peso to the US dollar rather than to gold. Nevertheless the Mexican government tried to stick to the strict rules of the gold standard and was also very eager to balance its budget. Thus it continued a severely deflationary policy even when it practically abandoned the gold standard in July 1931. At that time Mexico demonetised gold because its gold reserves were depleted. Finally the finance minister resigned at the end of 1931 and his predecessor returned to office. He followed a policy of easy money and reflated the economy. This he did by means of a very simple measure. He resumed the coining of silver pesos which also yielded a revenue to the government due to the collection of seignorage on the minting of coins.

Mexico's balance of payments was burdened by its debt service, but its balance of trade remained positive throughout the years of the depression. In the years from 1927 to 1929 this positive balance amounted to about $100 million, from 1930 to 1933 it was reduced to half that amount, but in 1934 it increased once more. Mexico was lucky because both silver and oil prices went up in 1934. The poor peasants and agricultural labourers, whose ranks were swelled by Mexican workers who lost their jobs in the United States, had to bear the brunt of the depression. Population increase also contributed to the reduction of per capita income which regained its 1925 level only in 1940. In spite of his spectacular expropriation of the foreign oil companies in 1938, President Cardenas (1934–40) could not do much for the alleviation of poverty in Mexico. He clashed with Great Britain and the United States due to this expropriation and appeared as a national hero because of that, but the immediate economic gains of this measure were rather modest. However, it certainly marked the peak of state intervention in Latin America in this crucial decade.

These six case studies of 'reactive' states have illustrated the common features as well as the differences in the fate of Latin American states in this period. We shall not discuss the many 'passive' states, because they do not provide examples of state intervention as induced by the depression. Several of them were ruled by dictators, but they were of the usual kind so often produced by Latin American states. Their actions did not illustrate state intervention but merely corruption, of the kind which President Leguia had practised in Peru.

11

CONTRASTS IN EAST ASIA
China and Japan

Just like the states of Latin America, China and Japan were sovereign states of the periphery which could conduct their own crisis management, but they were nevertheless dependent on the Western industrial powers, though in very different ways. China had a quasi-colonial status because the British controlled its essential ports and managed its customs offices, and they also had a major influence on Chinese monetary policy. At the same time China was a large agrarian country which was integrated in the world market only to a very limited extent. Moreover, it had a silver currency and had not joined the gold standard. This was of great significance in the early 1930s as we shall see in the next section of this chapter. In contrast with China, Japan was in full control of its international trade and its monetary policy and it had returned to the gold standard at the most inappropriate moment in 1930. Due to this fact and because of its great dependence on the American market, Japan was initially far more deeply affected by the depression than China. But whereas the depression reached China late and then lingered on, Japan was able to counteract its impact very quickly. Moreover, the transition from the depression to war happened much earlier in East Asia, because Japan attacked China in 1937 after already having invaded Manchuria in 1931.

THE DELAYED EMERGENCE OF THE CRISIS IN CHINA

China had experienced a major recession after the First World War. The silver price had fallen and Chinese entrepreneurs who had ordered investment goods abroad immediately after the war were caught unawares by the steep decline in the value of the Chinese silver currency. When the goods they had ordered arrived in China they were unable to pay for them. In February 1920 the exchange rate of the Chinese tael amounted to $1.48, by March 1921 it stood at $0.59; it then rose slightly and stood at $0.74 by the end of that year. At the same time exports had receded and the Chinese banking system was in no position to cope with this situation. China's negative balance of trade also affected the country's capacity to absorb silver and this led to a further fall in the price of silver which in turn depressed the exchange rate. China, like India, depended to a large extent on silver imports for its currency and their enormous demand determined the price of silver in the world market.

The Chinese currency system was, in fact, rather chaotic. In addition to silver, copper coins also circulated in large quantities. The old silver unit, the tael, was gradually replaced by the Chinese dollar, the yuan. In 1933 the tael ceased to be an official currency unit and the yuan prevailed, but the depreciation of silver was the same regardless of the denomination.

The positive effect of the depreciation of China's silver currency was that, like any devaluation, it encouraged import-substituting industries. As China had practically no independent control over its monetary policy or its exchange rate, this automatic devaluation was a boon in disguise. The Chinese textile industry expanded its production at that time. The export bonus associated with a devalued currency did not benefit China very much as the demand for Chinese goods in the world market was very limited. It took some time for China to increase its exports in the late 1920s.

The impact of the monetary contraction in the late 1920s and the early 1930s led once more to a steep fall in the price of silver. In 1927 the exchange rate of the Chinese yuan had amounted to $0.71, in 1930 and 1931 it stood at $0.21. In relation to the Japanese yen the depreciation was even more drastic: it receded from 1 yen per yuan in 1921 to 0.25 yen in 1931. But this time the depreciation of the silver currency had a surprising effect. The overseas Chinese had grown rich in the 1920s. They mostly lived in gold standard countries, and now they were able to buy much more silver for their money, which they then transferred to China. The officially recorded Chinese silver imports amounted to 165 million yuan in 1928 and 1929, and in 1930 imports worth 104 million yuan were recorded. In 1931 the flood of silver subsided, but nevertheless there were imports worth 71 million yuan. Additional silver probably reached China through other channels. The inflow of silver created a short lived boom in China at a time when other countries suffered from severe deflation. A good deal of the silver was invested in import-substituting industries which benefited once more from the protectionist effect of the depreciated silver currency. The Kuomintang government enhanced this protectionist effect by assessing customs duties in terms of gold rather than silver in 1930. This was done for purely fiscal reasons as the income from customs duties in silver had dwindled to such an extent that the government faced a severe decline in revenue. The Chinese textile industry had altogether 4 million spindles and 29,000 looms in 1929; in 1931 it had 5 million spindles and 43,000 looms. This phenomenal growth was due to the flow of silver. The big Japanese textile companies also participated in the investment boom. They quickly realised that under the prevailing conditions of automatic protectionism they had to establish textile mills in China producing for the Chinese home market. The Chinese government did not like this kind of Japanese penetration but could not do anything about it.

Chinese agriculture initially benefited from this protectionist effect of the depreciation of the silver currency. It was shielded against the steep fall of prices of agricultural produce in the world market. The relationship between landlord and tenant and creditor and agricultural debtor were not as monetised in China as in India. Rents and debts were mostly paid in kind. Grain credits usually had to be paid back by doubling the amount received in kind. Sharecropping was widespread, and many sharecroppers had contracts obliging them to deliver a fixed amount of rent in kind to their landlord. They could thus enhance the share left to them by intensifying their production, but, of course, there was also a stiff land revenue demand which did not leave much to the peasants. The distribution of land was highly uneven: about one tenth of rural households owned half of the cultivated land. Population increase had accentuated the scarcity of land and thus led to a more rigorous exploitation of tenants. The fact that the depreciation of the silver currency shielded the Chinese peasants against the fall in world market prices did not help them very much, because the prices of goods which they had to buy increased faster during the boom of 1929–31. However, the terms of trade for agriculture deteriorated in a big way only after 1933 when the depression hit China with a vengeance, and these terms of trade did not improve very much when prices for agricultural produce rose again after 1935.

Why did the depression hit China only in 1933 and then had an even greater impact on the national economy than elsewhere? The reason for this can be found once more in the development of the silver price. After Great Britain had abandoned the gold standard the silver price rose again and the overseas Chinese no longer sent silver to China but withdrew it. In 1932 silver imports stopped and silver exports began, but initially this export was on a modest scale. But in 1934 silver worth 257 million yuan was exported from China and probably more was smuggled out of the country. The cause for this was the American silver purchase policy which had been adopted as a result of the pressure of the mighty lobby of American producers of silver. The Silver Purchase Act passed in June 1934 obliged the government of the United States to hold a quarter of the currency reserves in silver. Within a few months the silver price had returned to the level of 1929 , i.e. it had doubled within a year. At this stage President Roosevelt wanted to fix the price of silver officially, but the silver lobby prevented him from doing that. From February to April 1935 the price of one ounce of silver increased from $0.55 to $0.81, i.e. by nearly 50 per cent. This meant a disastrous deflation for China and forced the Chinese government to abandon the silver standard and to go in for a radical currency reform.

The method by which this currency reform was achieved was so bold and devious that it is hard to believe that it could work. The Chinese government was already highly indebted and in order to place its government bonds at all it sold them at half the nominal price, which meant that it was burdened by a staggering debt service. The government had reached the end of its tether when the clever finance minister, Kung, made a virtue out of necessity and forced the creditors to obey the orders of the debtor. His opening gambit was as follows: he compelled the private Bank of China, with which he was connected, to buy up large amounts of government bonds and use this as a 'backing' for raising the stated amount of its paid up capital. In this way this bank was practically nationalised. He then instructed the Bank of China to cause the bankruptcy of all other private banks and then take them over, thus nationalising them, too. The trick by which this was done was a simple one. In China most banks issued their own bank notes in the absence of an authorised central bank. The banks which were already dominated by Kung bought up the bank notes of the other banks and presented them for encashment all at once. Of course, they could not pay up and had to join Kung's system. When he was thus in control of all the banks he was able to go ahead with his currency reform. He demonetised silver: all the banks had to hand over their silver to the government and the private possession of silver was prohibited. A new paper currency was issued instead. This could only work because the big British banks, which had a very powerful position in China, raised no objections to it. In fact, British advisers helped Kung to accomplish his coup. Once the currency was converted into a paper currency, Kung could get any amount of money printed and the government could pay its debts with that money. In this way the economy was reflated and prices rose once more. For the peasants this was not much of a consolation because the terms of trade for agriculture did not improve. Chaotic conditions prevailed in the countryside. Landlords hired gangs of men who would beat up recalcitrant tenants. Peasants fled from their land, perhaps only to join such a gang elsewhere. After 1937 there was war in China and as usual the peasants suffred most under its impact.

If one only looks at the small industrial sector of China one may come to the conclusion that the depression did not hit China at all, but meant a period of progress for Chinese industry. 'Revisionists' who want to reinterpret the history of the depression by pointing out that the periphery did not suffer under the impact of the depression but rather benefited from it, have used the case of China as an example which illustrates their claim. They highlight the fact that China did not experience a deflation at all, because the reduction in the circulation of the silver currency was compensated for by an increasing circulation of banknotes. From 1933 to 1935 silver currency in circulation was reduced from 2.2 to 1.7 billion yuan, but the circulation of banknotes increased by 0.5 billion yuan. Bank deposits increased by 1.2 billion yuan in this period. Thus the export of silver apparently did not affect China at all. One could ask the revisionists why prices fell in China in 1934–35 and why the government was forced to go in for a currency reform if the export of silver did not affect the country at all. The revisionists also argue that silver exports after 1934 meant a profit for China and increased the purchasing power of the Chinese masses. These were exactly the same arguments which were used by the American silver lobby to justify their stand. We may remember that the British colonial rulers also justified their non-interference with Indian gold exports at that time by pointing out that the Indians sold that gold because they got a good price for it. The question remains, of course, who actually benefited from the de-hoarding of silver and gold? The peasants had to part with their savings, but those who participated in the trade in silver and gold were the real beneficiaries of this development. The Chinese bank deposits mentioned above were certainly not those of peasants but of urban people who prospered during the depression. Of course, even if such de-hoarding hurts the peasants but leads to investment in the national industry and thus to a spurt of economic growth which will finally also benefit agriculture, it may be welcomed from a general economic point of view. But China did not experience such a growth spurt. Japan was in a much better position to get ahead in this way, but as we shall see it had its own problems which were accentuated by the impact of the depression.

CRISIS MANAGEMENT IN JAPAN

Japan had joined the international gold standard in 1897 and had left it again in September 1916 due to the war. After Great Britain returned to the gold standard in 1925 at the prewar parity, Japan wanted to follow this example but could not do so because of economic problems which forced it to stick to a gold export embargo which was incompatible with returning to the gold standard. Japan's economic problems were caused by several factors. In the postwar sequence of boom and recession, Japan had used its dollar reserves saved during the war in order to support the yen. The earthquake of 1923 completely upset the government's monetary policy. It had to finance the reconstruction and to accept a depreciation of the yen. But this had boosted Japanese exports: silk exports to the United States, in particular, increased very rapidly. When Japan was drifting into inflation, the government exported gold, the value of the yen rose and internal prices fell. As a consequence of this deflationary policy many banks failed in Japan in 1927 and the government had to revise its monetary policy once more and to postpone the return to the gold standard.

In 1929 a new government was formed and the finance minister, Inouye, returned to an orthodox policy of balancing the budget. He wanted to lift the embargo on the export of gold and was

115

encouraged in this by a positive balance of trade. So in January 1930 his aim was reached and Japan returned to the gold standard only a few months before all hell broke loose. Inouye tried to support the yen, pursued a deflationary policy and lost much of Japan's gold reserves while internal prices fell steeply, in some instances even before they fell to the same extent in the world market. We have seen how the fall of the rice price in Japan in October 1930 affected the world market price of rice, leading to serious consequences in India. Inouye nevertheless did not think of a devaluation of the yen, not even when the British abandoned the gold standard in September 1931. He looked on when Japan's gold reserves rapidly flowed out of the country, as foreign speculators were convinced that Japan would have to follow the British precedent very soon. The great Japanese firm Mitsui was deeply involved in these kinds of speculations. In December 1931 the government fell, Japan left the gold standard, and the yen was permitted to float like the pound. In this way the yen depreciated by 60 per cent in 1932.

These events were paralleled by deep social tensions in Japan. The army had emerged as a decisive political force, defending the interests of the peasants against the big corporations. It also followed an aggressive policy of expansion abroad and had invaded Manchuria in September 1931 without the approval of the Japanese government. The army was also behind the murders of Inouye and of Baron Dan, the head of the Mitsui corporation, in the spring of 1932. They were, so to speak, 'executed' for betraying the interests of the Japanese people. Finance minister Takahashi, Inouye's successor, who piloted Japan through the years of the depression, was also murdered by army officers in 1936. It was clearly very dangerous to be in charge of Japan's financial affairs in this crucial period.

In the four years during which he was in charge of the finance ministry, Takahashi followed a policy which was to some extent like that of Schacht in Germany, and he also followed a pattern similar to that set by Great Britain with the Exchange Equalisation Account. The government issued a large number of government bonds and then redeemed them in keeping with the needs of a stable monetary policy. But there was the problem of the rising expenditure on rearmament which claimed almost half of the budget by 1936. When Takahashi wanted to stop the further increase of this type of expenditure, his days were numbered.

The devaluation of the yen meant an export bonus and an encouragement of import-substituting industries. As the decline of the yen was so dramatic and Japanese industry was very efficient, Japanese products soon swamped the world market. There was a strong feeling among competitors abroad that this was a flagrant case of exchange dumping motivated by the demand for foreign exchange for Japanese rearmament. But this export drive had the effect of diversifying Japanese production and getting away from the earlier dependence on silk exports to America. This type of export had been the major one before 1929 and once it had collapsed it proved to be difficult to revive. The export of raw silk had a share of 36 per cent of Japanese exports in 1929, but in 1934 it had receded to 13 per cent. On the other hand the export of cotton textiles which amounted to 19 per cent in 1929 had increased to 23 per cent in 1934. Raw silk was a product of Japanese agriculture, but the raw cotton had to be imported from abroad at a high cost due to the depreciation of the yen. In order to produce cotton textiles at a profit, Japanese workers had to be exploited rigorously. Critics called this 'hunger export'. The Japanese denied this, but it was true. The big Japanese corporations (*zaibatsu*) sub-contracted most of their work and relied on numerous small suppliers onto whose shoulders they could shift the burden whenever the demand for their products receded. The textile mills worked with the most modern machinery but with a workforce of young girls who were paid minimal wages. They usually lived in a kind of barracks on the premises of the mill, and they were replaced by new recruits after a few years. The Japanese peasants were so poor that they had to sell their daughters, many of them ending up in the brothels of the big cities. Compared to that fate, work in a textile mill seemed to be a better option.

The purchasing power of the masses did not increase under such circumstances. Wages stagnated and the income of the rural population increased only very little after the depreciation of the yen and the recovery of the internal price level. The import-substituting industry of Japan was not primarily producing consumer goods for the home market, it was the heavy industry preparing for rearmament which was most prominent. Japan had made some progress in the field of industrialisation even before the 1930s and therefore new industries making electrical goods and machine tools could also prosper. Inputs for these industries, which needed to be imported, had to be paid for by increasing exports. One could speak of a self-exploitation of Japan in the interest of industrial progress and military expansionism. It was an irony of fate that the army which posed as the advocate of half of the Japanese population, which depended on agriculture and which was highly distrustful of urban capitalism, nevertheless pressed for industrial progress aimed at rearmament. The big corporations which the army professed to hate, such as Mitsui, Mitsubishi and Sumitomo profited from this development, and their ranks were swelled by others (e.g. Nissan) in the 1930s. The phenomenon of a redistribution of income in favour of the rich which could be observed in other countries at that time was certainly also apparent in Japan.

The great achievements of Japan in mastering the crisis, the radical devaluation, the skilful open market operations which increased prices without leading to inflation, the impressive industrial growth and the success of Japanese exports – all this has to be seen in the context of the sufferings of workers and peasants, of social tensions, rising militarism and aggressive expansionism abroad. China was at the receiving end of this development: the Japanese army invaded Manchuria in 1931, then Japanese firms penetrated China, and in 1937 Japanese troops conquered large parts of that country. Some Western economists have been fond of recommending the Japanese precedent to developing countries all over the world. Of course, they mostly have the peaceful postwar Japan in mind when making such recommendations: they forget about the preceding period with its painful self-exploitation and the consequences of an aggressive militarism which had motivated the rapid industrialisation of the country.

Finally it should be mentioned that the demographic development of Japan was different from that of the Western industrial countries at that time. Whereas those countries experienced a steep decline of the birth rate, the Japanese population grew very substantially in the 1920s and 1930s. In 1920 there were 56 million Japanese, in 1930 64 million, and by 1940 there were 72 million. This amounted to a rate of increase of 14.3 per cent in the first decade and 12.5 per cent in the second one. The birth rate decreased from 35 per thousand in 1925 to 32 per thousand in 1935. The death rate declined in the same period from 20 to 17 per thousand. This meant that the decisive point in the demographic transition was reached in the depression years and not thirty years earlier as in Europe. It is possible that the depression directly contributed to the reduction of the Japanese birth rate. As has been explained before, decline of the death rate is usually followed by a reduction in the birth rate after some time, but this is not necessarily so, as shown by many countries in which the birth rate did not decline. This means that other factors must intervene which cause the birth rate to follow the death rate in its downward trend. The shock of the depression may have been such a factor in Japan, but the effect would be felt only after thirty years. In the depression years Japan was still a rapidly growing nation and the German slogan of 'a nation without space' could very well apply to Japan and encourage its aggressive expansionism.

12

REACTIONS TO THE
DEPRESSION IN
SOUTHEAST ASIA

The countries of this region were mostly colonies of Western powers at the time of the depression. They produced raw produce such as sugar, rubber and hemp, and also rice. Import-substituting industries were practically denied to these countries. Agrarian relations and revenue systems differed a great deal, so the impact of the depression made itself felt in very different ways. But as a general rule we may state that wherever the colonial rulers collected poll taxes in addition to the land revenue, the conflict potential was particularly high, the more so as the colonial governments could not afford to be lenient in collecting such taxes, as they were hard pressed to balance their budgets. Only in the Philippines, where the American colonial rulers were lax in their tax collection, were there hardly any conflicts. But in Burma and Vietnam, where the British and the French collected poll taxes without pity, they faced bloody riots. These will be described in subsequent sections of this chapter. Initially we shall turn to the contrasting patterns of reactions to the depression by the two major sugar producing countries: Java and the Philippines.

JAVA AND THE PHILIPPINES: CONTRASTING PATTERNS OF SUGAR EXPORTS

Under the influence of Dutch colonial rule, Java had emerged as one of the biggest sugar exporters in the world. From 1928 to 1930 annual sugar exports had amounted to 3 million tonnes: India imported a great deal of that sugar, but as we have seen before, this import was rapidly reduced by a prohibitive tariff. In the years from 1933 to 1936 Javanese sugar exports declined from 1.4 million to 1 million tonnes. But the decline in the volume of exports was also accompanied by a steep fall in the price of sugar so that by 1936 earnings from sugar export amounted only to 10 per cent of 1928 earnings. Workers in the sugar refineries faced unemployment and had to return to the rice fields. The phenomenon of 'agrarian involution' so graphically described by Clifford Geertz, was of increasing importance in the depression years. Work sharing in agriculture helps to absorb labour, the more so as rice cultivation responds to higher labour inputs so that higher yields can feed more people. The urban people of Java experienced a growth of their real income during the depression, unless they were unemployed and did not return to the countryside.

Java should have provided an ideal location for a strong anti-colonial movement at that time, but the Dutch governed it with an iron fist. A communist uprising in 1928 had been suppressed, and in December 1929, even before the impact of the depression hit Java, Sukarno and several other nationalists had been arrested. They spent the years of the depression in jail. Governor General de Jonge who ruled the Netherlands East Indies from 1931 to 1936 was a tough autocrat who was backed by the Dutch government at home.

The Philippines had an entirely different fate. American colonial rule was very mild, most government posts were occupied by indigenous people, and the Americans themselves were hardly in evidence. Thus protests could only have been directed against the indigenous elite, but this elite did not face much trouble because the American connection proved to be very beneficial for the Philippines in the years of the depression, as they had privileged access to the American market. Thus annual sugar exports grew from 0.7 million tonnes (1929–31) to 1 million tonnes (1932–34). The import potential of the Philippines was hardly affected. Import-substituting industries did not emerge because of the access to the American market and, in addition, Japanese goods were available cheaply. One export commodity was affected by the depression, the famous Manila hemp, but the peasants who grew it could return to rice cultivation. The fact that the colonial rulers were lax in their tax collection contributed to rural peace. Moreover, the relationship between landlord and tenant was still rather that of patron and client in the Philippines. Thus there was no conflict potential whatever.

THE CRISIS OF THE RICE EXPORT ECONOMY OF BURMA

In striking contrast with the quiet agrarian involution of Javanese rice growers, the peasants of Burma rose in rebellion under the impact of the depression. The fertile plains of Lower Burma were the premier rice exporting region of Asia. In the years preceding the depression 2 million tonnes of rice were exported annually from this region; the value of these exports amounted to 200 million rupees per year. Agrarian relations had changed under the impact of this export economy. The landlords were no longer the old style patrons, but rapacious absentees who lived in town. Nearly half of these landlords were not Burmese but Chettiars, South Indian money lenders who also controlled the rice market. They exacted the rent in kind and adopted devious methods when measuring rice for this purpose, for which the peasants hated them. Actually rent paid in kind should not have been affected by the depression, but almost all peasants were indebted and creditors and grain dealers accounted the rents in kind in terms of their value in cash – and the same was true of the debt service. On top of all this the peasants had to pay a stiff poll tax which was equivalent to an amount of rice with which the peasant could have fed his family for two to three months. The poor people were hit hardest in this way, as their very survival was at stake. This increased their solidarity and they readily turned to a charismatic leader and rose in rebellion.

In December 1930 this rebellion erupted under the leadership of Saya San, a devout Buddhist who claimed to be a just king under whose rule no taxes would have to be paid. Buddhism actually teaches non-violence, but Saya San nevertheless preached violent resistance to injustice. The proximate cause of the rebellion was the impending collection of the poll tax. A peasant delegation had petitioned the government for its remittance, but the government had declined their request. December 1930 was a crucial month: the fall of the rice price in Great Britain in November was already known in Burma and the money lenders refused to give credit to the peasants for the payment of the poll tax. Hitherto the money lenders had profited from the fact that the peasants were compelled to pay poll tax a few weeks before the winter harvest, as they could then dictate the price of rice to them when they had to pay their debts after the harvest. The poll tax was actually an export

122

promoting device as it forced the peasants to market as much rice as possible. The government also levied duties on the export of rice, so it benefited twice from this pressure on the peasants. The whole system worked well only as long as the going was good and the money lenders provided credit to satisfy the tax collector. If the money lender refused to provide credit and demanded interest on the previous debt, while the tax collector pounced on the peasant, a clash was inevitable. Peasant solidarity is difficult to achieve under normal circumstances, but if thousands of peasants face the same grim situation and stand with their backs to the wall, solidarity grows all of a sudden.

The rebellion led by Saya San lasted for nearly two years. The British had to send troops to crush it, but since almost all districts of Lower Burma were affected, they could not cope with it very quickly. Only when they captured and executed Saya San in 1932 were they able to put an end to the rebellion. In spite of all this unrest, rice exports from Lower Burma continued almost undiminished. In 1931 2 million tonnes were exported, in 1932 1.6 million tonnes and in both 1933 and 1934, 1.4 million tonnes a year. The value of rice exports declined steeply due to the fall in prices. While the proceeds from rice exports had amounted to 220 million rupees in 1930, this receded to 150 million rupees for the same volume of exports in 1931. When in 1933 both volume and value of rice exports had declined, the proceeds amounted to only 90 million rupees. It is amazing that the peasants still produced for export under such conditions rather that reverting to subsistence agriculture. But they still had to pay taxes and were subjected to debt service and thus could not withdraw from export production. The rebellion had not improved their fate: after it had been crushed they had to bow their heads again and continue their work as usual.

PEASANT RESISTANCE IN VIETNAM

In Vietnam a peasant rebellion had been precipitated by the collection of the poll tax even before Saya San's rebellion in Burma. This rebellion was not initially a reaction to the fall in the rice price, it was due to a disaster of a different kind. In the central region of Vietnam (Northern Annam) rainfall was always precarious, and this time the rains had failed completely and there was a famine. The soils of this area are of a peculiar type, they yield a rich harvest when the rainfall is good, but when it is deficient the soil is like baked clay and yields nothing at all. In the first half of 1930 the rice price was still high and was even supported by the famine, but the prices for cash crops such as tobacco and hemp had already fallen and the peasants could not pay the poll tax. This triggered off a rebellion which was at first rather ineffective due to a lack of leadership. It was only when it was in full swing that urban communists joined the fray and organised the peasants in soviet-style peasant councils. The urban educated elite of this area had always had a reputation for rebelliousness and it is perhaps no accident that Ho Chi Minh was born here. The fate of the rebellious peasants was the same as that of the Burmese rebels: they were ruthlessly suppressed. The Vietnamese rebellion was already over in 1931. Probably this served as a discouraging example for this as well as other regions when the fall in the rice price really hit Vietnam in that same year.

To make matters worse, in 1931 the French colonial government had tied the local currency, the piastre, to the French franc, which had returned to the gold standard in 1928. This was obviously done in order to protect French investments in Vietnam. This unfortunate measure priced Vietnamese rice out of the world market and accordingly led to an even further decline of the internal rice price. Wherever possible the peasants withdrew into 'agrarian involution'. However, debt service became more burdensome due to the overvalued piastre and it was only the devaluation of the franc in 1936 that eased the situation in Vietnam.

North and South Vietnam developed along different lines under the impact of the depression and this was of major consequence for future developments. In South Vietnam the big landlords consolidated their position and evicted their tenants, depressing them to the status of landless labour. In North Vietnam, which was an area of peasant smallholders, suppressed protest was smouldering and was later on articulated by the communist Vietminh, who had been actively involved in the rebellion of 1930.

These case studies of reactions to the depression in various Southeast Asian countries have shown a rather complicated pattern. The specific conditions of colonial rule and of agrarian relations, of land use patterns and ecological structure, as well as the degree of dependence on production for export gave rise to a variety of responses to the challenge of the depression. Violent rebellions occurred only where shortsighted colonial rulers provided reasons for them by collecting taxes ruthlessly at an inopportune moment. In general the peasants withdrew into the shell of 'agrarian involution' and suffered silently. The articulation of peasant protest of the kind seen under Gandhi in India was not available to the peasants of Southeast Asia.

13

THE FATE OF AFRICA

Africa was almost completely under colonial rule at the time of the Great Depression and served as a source of agricultural produce and of ores and minerals for its masters. In a few areas white settlers owned large estates and were dependent on African labour, but in most parts of Africa the production and marketing of agricultural produce were in the hands of the Africans. Unlike in India where revenue administration and titles in land were major preoccupations of the colonial power, land law was for the most part of no concern to the colonial rulers of Africa. They left this to customary law, though in many places customary law turned into 'lawyer's customary law', i.e. a hybrid breed of original custom and what the lawyers made of it when presenting cases in colonial courts. Taxes were mostly poll taxes or export taxes, therefore the colonial rulers had no reason to bother about the administration of land revenue or to interfere with the pattern of landholding.

The export of agricultural produce was in the hands of large European trading companies. Similarly the exploitation of mines and the export of ores and minerals were controlled by European companies. Just as in Latin America, such companies had to bear the brunt of the Great Depression. Africans were only affected to the extent that they lost their jobs and had to turn to agriculture in order to make a living. Many parts of Africa were still at the stage of subsistence agriculture and were therefore not immediately affected by the slump. But colonial rulers collected poll taxes and thus the African peasants had to market some of their produce in order to pay those taxes. Moreover, the colonial rulers used these poll taxes as a means of extracting a cheap supply of such produce from the peasantry. As we shall see, the Belgian Congo was a particularly glaring example of this type of practice.

Industrialisation and import substitution were impossible for most African countries at that time. Egypt, which has been described earlier, was an exception to this rule. Revisionists who try to show that the Great Depression had a positive effect on the periphery find it difficult to prove their case in Africa. The only examples which they can quote are not incidences of import substitution but of the processing of the output of mines, e.g. copper in Katanga and in Northern Rhodesia. In this there was some progress in the years of the depression, because costs could be cut in this way. The production of gold was also stepped up in those years. The white settlers in Kenya and Southern Rhodesia, however, had a very bad time and left much of their land to African peasants. This will be described in detail later on.

CURRENCIES AND COMPETITION

All colonies depended entirely on the currencies of their rulers, who did not mint their own currency here as they did in India. As Great Britain and Portugal had left the gold standard in 1931 while other European countries had stuck to it, this affected the prices of agricultural produce and enhanced competition, particularly if the same type of produce was grown in adjacent territories which were ruled by different colonial rulers. Under such circumstances peasants were sometimes pressed very hard to grow cash crops which no longer gave them any returns. Indebtedness or harsh taxation were used as instruments of pressure. There was resistance to it, but as political organisations did not yet exist and the coercive power of the colonial rulers was far superior, open rebellion was quickly crushed. At the most some quasi-religious movements or new cults gave an expression to the feelings of the people. The authority of 'chieftains' appointed by the colonial rulers was strengthened in the depression years, but in the long run their authority suffered as they were seen as collaborators and when the colonies became independent they no longer qualified as leaders of the people. These political consequences of the impact of the depression will be discussed in Chapter 14.

Even if we restrict our analysis to Black Africa and leave out Northern Africa, we have to deal with a large number of different territories which we cannot study in detail. Just as in the case of Latin America we shall select only a a few exemplary cases. We shall begin with the West African colonies: the Ivory Coast, the

Gold Coast (Ghana), Togo and Nigeria. These were British and French colonies respectively which produced more or less the same kind of tropical goods for export. We shall then devote special attention to the Belgian Congo which suffered a particularly harsh kind of exploitation in the depression years. Finally we shall turn to colonies with white settlers such as Kenya and Southern Rhodesia (Zimbabwe). This somewhat arbitrary selection more or less reflects the state of research as not much is known about the depression years in many African territories. Even the case studies presented here are based mostly on very slender evidence. It is particularly difficult to obtain information about the fate of the African peasants whereas that of the large European companies and of the colonial governments is much better documented.

WEST AFRICA: AFRICAN PRODUCERS AND EUROPEAN TRADING COMPANIES

The four West African colonies mentioned above produced a rather limited number of export items, mostly palm oil and cocoa. The producers were African peasants, the exporters European companies. Some African traders served as intermediaries. The peasants did not derive much profit from this production, as the lion's share of the profits went to the European companies. Due to the First World War the German trading companies had been eliminated and the British and French companies, which had acquired a kind of monopoly during the war, had entrenched themselves even more firmly after it ended. The terms of trade for the African peasants deteriorated after 1914. The First World War had pushed up import prices while export prices did not increase to the same extent. The European companies were engaged in both the import and the export trade. During the depression import prices fell more steeply than export prices, because they had been maintained at a high level ever since the war.

The depression confronted the European companies with a dilemma. They had to maintain their profits from trade and tried to shift the burden of the depression to the African peasants. At the same time they had to pay them enough to prevent them from relinquishing production of the respective cash crops altogether. As importers they were also interested in maintaining the purchasing power of their African customers. They put pressure on the colonial administration to lower export taxes and argued that they did so in the interest of the African peasants. But if the colonial rulers lowered the export tax they were compelled to enhance the poll tax. The trading companies welcomed the enhancement of the poll tax as it forced the peasants to produce for the market. If the peasants rebelled, the colonial rulers had to put down such rebellions and the trading companies could deny all responsibility for this and continue to make profits even in the worst years of the depression. The case of the French Ivory Coast illustrates this point very well. It was rated as an economically dynamic colony, which exported mostly cocoa and palm kernels. The French government at home pressed the colonial administration to push up production at a time when the peasants would have liked to stop production altogether because of the fall in prices. The trading companies continued business as usual until the autumn of 1931, because they maintained their profits as the burden of the depression was completly shifted to the African producers. When Great Britain left the gold standard while France stuck to it, competition increased. At this stage the French companies began to clamour for a reduction of export taxes.

The colonial administration yielded to this pressure and lowered the export taxes but had to enhance the poll tax, although there had been a significant increase in that tax from 1925 to 1929. Every person above the age of 14 years had to pay poll tax. In the 1920s the peasants could still afford to pay this tax and therefore the colonial administration had been able to enhance it without facing trouble. With the onset of the depression the government should have reduced this tax, but instead it collected it without remission and tried to increase it even more. The purchasing power of the peasants was reduced in this way. Many of them fled to the towns and settled in slums.

The adjacent British Gold Coast faced other problems. There was no poll tax there at all – the export tax was the only revenue the government collected. The cocoa producers were bound by contract to the trading companies. When the depression hit them they held up their deliveries to the companies. But in the autumn of 1931 the British departure from the gold standard gave the Gold Coast cocoa producers a competitive edge over their French neighbours and exports increased again. Possibly the African peasants there were better off than those in other colonies in the depression years.

Togo, earlier a German colony and now a French mandate terrority, was in a peculiar position in the 1930s. As a mandate territory Togo was not permitted to levy high export taxes and therefore its capital, Lome, was a smuggler's paradise. Cocoa and other produce of the neighbouring colonies were shipped via Lome. The Ewe peasants of Southern Togo did not grow cash crops, but instead produced food crops for their neighbours who specialised in growing cash crops only. The trade in food crops was entirely in African hands. But all this was swept away by the impact of the depression. Moreover, in 1931 the export taxes levied in Lome and in the neighbouring ports were adjusted to each other and this removed Lome's attractiveness as an entrepôt for smugglers. On top of this the poll tax, which had only amounted to a quarter of the revenue income of the colonial administration in earlier years, was raised to such an extent that by 1934 half of the revenue was derived from this source. There were riots in 1933 which the colonial rulers suppressed, but obviously they had learned their lesson and in subsequent years the poll tax was reduced.

In the large British colony of Nigeria there were several agrarian regions with different cash crops. In Southeastern Nigeria palm oil products predominated, while in Western Nigeria, around Lagos, cocoa production had been pushed ahead in the 1920s. In Northern Nigeria peanut production had made rapid progress. Before the First World War about 80 per cent of the Nigerian palm kernel harvest was exported to Germany, because it was the only country which had installed the machines for making palm oil and also the only country where oil cakes were used as fodder. After the war Lever Brothers had entered this market and had practically monopolised it. In contrast to other export products there was also a demand for palm oil in the African home market. Therefore the producers were not as totally dependent on the export market as those producing cocoa and peanuts. Nigeria, like all the other colonies, was affected by the deterioration of the terms of trade imposed on African peasants since the war. In addition, the introduction of a poll tax in Southern Nigeria had been decided upon in 1927 and by 1931 its collection was in full swing. This caused unrest. Even earlier, in December 1929, the 'War of the Ibo Women' had attracted much attention and the authorities were forced to reduce the poll tax.

While the colonial administration taxed the Africans to such an extent that they were left with hardly any cash, there was also a struggle for survival among the European trading companies and only a few of them remained in business. The establishment of the United Africa Company in 1929 set the pace. Only monopsonist practices guaranteed the survival of the trading companies. But all this was surpassed by the practices of the Belgians in their Congo colony where they introduced a rigorous system of forced cultivation.

FORCED CULTIVATION IN THE BELGIAN CONGO

There was an earlier tradition of forced cultivation in this colony. When it was still the personal property of the Belgian king, the poll tax had to be paid in terms of forced labour. Only when the Belgian government took over the colony in 1910, was the poll tax commuted to cash. This, of course, was also a burden for the peasants, but in the 1920s they had not been exploited too much, because mines and plantations had prospered and had yielded a good revenue income. Before the depression set in, 60 per cent of all exports were products of the mines. The rest consisted of palm kernels and cocoa. Both types of exports were severely hit by the depression. The Europeans connected with the mines and with trade left the colony in a hurry, because it proved to be particularly vulnerable. The colonial administration now depended more than ever before on the poll tax. In 1930 it had amounted only to one sixth of revenue income, by 1932 it amounted to one quarter. The producers of palm kernels were particularly affected by the fall in prices and were hard pressed by the tax. There were rebellions which were put down brutally. In order to push export production and also to secure their revenue income the authorities reverted to the old sytem of forced labour. They told the peasants what to grow and dictated the prices. The pressure of taxation compelled the peasants to obey. Anybody who failed to do his duty was prosecuted. In their reports the colonial officers stated that they were educating the natives to devote themselves to agriculture, and thus tried to justify the brutal system of forced labour which was financially successful in the short run but reduced the exploited peasants to complete poverty. Since Africans could neither buy nor sell land and since trade was entirely in the hands of the European companies, there was no scope for the growth of an indigenous middle class in this system.

One reason for the financial success of the system was the planned diversification of the production of export crops. Cotton, peanuts, oil palms, rice, coffee and maize were grown in the regions best suited to the specific crop. The administration thus converted the colony into a diversified plantation under unified management. Cotton exports trebled from 1929 to 1937 and palm oil exports doubled. All colonial rulers tried to overcome the depression by putting the burden on African shoulders, but the Belgians proved to be the masters of this game.

WHITE SETTLERS AND BLACK PEASANTS: KENYA AND SOUTHERN RHODESIA (ZIMBABWE)

A very special case of coping with the depression was represented by Kenya, where white settlers carried on a modern type of capitalist agriculture in the so-called 'white highlands', where they had prospered in the 1920s. About 1,200 large landholders owned 1.5 million hectares altogether, of which they cultivated only 85,000 hectares. In 1929 there were 2,000 landholders who owned 2.5 million hectares, of which they cultivated 300,000 hectares. The slump hit them hard, but they did not leave Africa in a hurry as the Belgians had done. On the contrary, they expanded cultivation until 1931. It then receded until 1936 and increased somewhat in the subsequent two years. By that time the number of settlers (1,900) and the cultivated area (250,000 hectares) attained once more the level reached in 1928. Each of these large landholders cultivated about 150 hectares. They were able to weather the storm of the depression, but they could do so only by exploiting African labour.

This exploitation was organised in different ways. The plantation owners who grew coffee, sisal or tea depended on African labourers, whom they paid very low wages. Colonial legislation had seen to it that the breach of a labour contract could be prosecuted like a criminal offence. Anyone who entered such a contract was practically a slave. Other white settlers grew maize and they had different problems. Maize no longer had any market. At first the colonial administration had subsidised the production of maize and had almost gone bankrupt by doing so. Then a Maize Control Act was supposed to be introduced – just like in Southern Rhodesia, as will be shown later on – but this would have forced the other white settlers to pay higher wages to their labourers, who lived on maize, so they prevented the passing of the act. Thus the maize growers were left only with the alternative of letting out their land to their African labourers who were turned into tenants but could be treated as 'squatters' when the landowners wanted to get rid of them. These African tenants made the most of their family labour, and the landlords were, so to speak, riding on their backs throughout the depression. When prices rose again and the white settlers wanted to evict the 'squatters' they rose in rebellion and the Mau-Mau movement took its course.

The 'white highlands' were part of the tribal lands of the Kikuyu who had earlier practised a rather primitive but extensive cultivation of these lands and had then settled on the periphery of the area claimed by the white settlers – or had become 'squatters'. As has been mentioned earlier, the land occupied by the settlers far exceeded the cultivated area, so most Africans living there were practically 'squatters'. The rigorous collection of the poll tax compelled the Africans to work as labourers on the white man's fields. The 'squatters' who had been turned into 'tenants' had to pay poll tax to the government and rent to their landlords. The revenue income from the poll tax amounted to about £500,000 sterling. Kenya had about 3 million inhabitants at that time of which, at the most, 1 million must have been adult males paying poll tax. There was no reduction of this tax during the years of the depression, and the colonial administration even introduced an additional hut tax for women. In the polygamous Kikuyu society, a man usually had several wives, each entitled to a hut of her own, so this hut tax was considered to be particularly unfair. The Masai herdsmen who were considered to be wealthy and would not work on agricultural land had to pay a higher poll tax. Many of them had to sell their cattle in the years of the depression.

In contrast to the cultivation system practised in the Belgian Congo, the Africans in Kenya were free to decide what they wanted to cultivate. Only coffee growing was prohibited, as this was a privilege of the white settlers. The African peasants could thus make a modest amount of money by selling food crops or by growing acacia trees whose bark was used for tanning. But it would be an exaggeration to state that the Kikuyu in this way started a new type of production for the market. The Kenyan peasants at least had the benefit of entering the depression years without being indebted, but this was only due to colonial legislation which severely restricted the granting of credit to Africans. The only land mortgage bank in Kenya did not provide credit to Africans, but wasted its capital on bailing out bankrupt white settlers. The Mau-Mau movement which emerged after the Second World War was a reaction against decades of exploitation, not an expression of the assertiveness of a new agrarian bourgeoisie.

The lot of the African peasants in Southern Rhodesia (Zimbabwe) was even worse than that of the Kenyans. Southern Rhodesia had about 1 million inhabitants in 1930. The poll tax amounted to £1 sterling and was thus very high indeed. There were white settlers here, too, who depended on African labour. They mostly grew maize and were able to lobby the colonial administration so as to get a Maize Control Act passed (1931, amended 1934). This act restricted the area of cultivation in order to control output. The total production of maize was to be procured by the government at a fixed price. Local consumers had to buy maize at a price well above the export price. Maize procurement was regulated in such a way that only the white maize growers profited from it. Africans who still dared to grow the crop had to sell it below the export price.

In adopting these measures the government had shot itself in the foot, because it could no longer collect poll tax from peasants who could not produce for the market. In some areas the district officers helped the African peasants to market their produce because this was the only way in which they could collect any tax at all and preserve the foundations of colonial rule. But in most places the depression ruined the African peasants and turned them into proletarians. The white settlers liked this development as they depended on African labour. The increasing impoverishment forced the government to commute their poll tax demand. Africans could work for twenty-three days on road construction instead of paying their annual tax assessment. This offer was taken up to such an extent that the government had to withdraw it. The old system of fines or imprisonment for debt was reintroduced in order to force the tax payers to settle their accounts.

All case studies show that colonial rulers and European trading companies were able to shift the burden of the depression to the African peasants. If those peasants tried to go back to subsistence agriculture they were debarred from it by tax demands and debt service. Wherever white settlers were involved, the Africans suffered even more, because they were pressed into service in order to help the settlers survive the depression. The economic crisis turned into a general crisis of colonial rule. Put under undue pressure by settlers and/or trading companies and faced with a decline in revenues, the colonial administration could scarcely manage to preserve law and order. The Belgian colonial rulers solved this problem by reintroducing forced labour, but in doing so they also ruined any prospects for a peaceful decolonisation. Of course, they were not contemplating decolonisation at that time, and perhaps believed that they could rule for ever.

14

THE POLITICAL CONSEQUENCES OF THE DEPRESSION

Fascism in Europe, populism in Latin America and freedom movements in the colonies

Almost everywhere, the depression hit the poor harder than the rich. Peasants, unemployed workers, small traders – they all suffered from severe deprivation. Debtors were faced with debt service at constant rates whereas their incomes had declined considerably. The only beneficiaries were those who received fixed salaries as they could enjoy cheap food and a drop in the prices of most consumer goods. Those who were confronted with the depression, including politicians and economists, had no idea why all this had happened, and looked for scapegoats. Speculators, bankers and monopoly capitalists were blamed for the depression. Since scapegoats have to be named there were even more concrete allegations: the people in Wall Street, the Jews, etc. were at fault. Some people went a step further and constructed conspiracy theories. There must have been a deep laid plan behind all this to fool the people and to destroy their livelihood. In many countries this led to the rise of populism. Politicians tried to portray themselves as protectors of the people against these sinister forces. They usually had no idea of economic affairs, but they made up for this by impressive rhetoric. Wherever the political system had been dominated by a small upper class in previous years, such populist leaders managed to seize power and to cling to it by making arrangements with the upper classes without depending on them too much.

Populist politicians usually enlarged the apparatus of the state and introduced all kinds of controls and public works programmes in order to cope with unemployment. The scale of this kind of politics reached from Roosevelt's New Deal to the compulsory measures of fascist dictators. The specific course which this kind of politics would take in different countries depended on the historical preconditions. In political systems with a great deal of stability, such as Great Britain, populism did not have much of a chance. In some countries social democratic parties came to power without breaking with the established political process (Sweden in 1932, France in 1936). But in many countries new types of political systems emerged during the depression, for instance in Latin America and in Central and Southern Europe. It would go beyond the scope of this book to review all of them. We shall also skip a discussion of the New Deal, because it did not really change the American political system.

Populism is, of course, a rather vague term. Some political scientists use it merely as a synonym for demagoguery, others would even attach this label to political systems characterised by a dictatorial or quasi-dictatorial regime which depends on state intervention in the economy and the repression of any kind of opposition. Populist regimes of this type usually do not subject themselves to the democratic process and can be dislodged only by a coup. They tend to argue that they represent the real aspirations of the people and project some half-baked ideology. In this they differ from the conservative law-and-order dictatorships which are satisfied with being in power and feel no need to justify their position. In the period of the depression conservative dictatorships would not do. There were enormous problems which had to be faced and the people expected a problem solving approach from their leaders. Populism projects itself as a problem solving initiative: the political form it takes may differ according to the historical preconditions, but its general features are similar and they emerged almost everywhere in the years of the depression.

In the African and Asian colonies of Western powers populism assumed the form of anti-imperialist freedom movements. There was no need to look for other scapegoats here, the colonial rulers were blamed for everything. They had been hit by the depression themselves, but that did not interest African and Asian nationalists. They could always point to colonial measures which had exacerbated the impact of the depression and had clearly revealed that the colonial overlords did not care for the people they ruled. Fascism was no option for the colonies as they could

137

not yet determine their political fate, but colonial freedom movements could evince sympathies for the fascists, as they were enemies of the colonial rulers. The old rule that the enemy of my enemy is my friend proved to be rather dangerous in this context. But the fascist regimes showed hardly any inclination to cash in on this kind of sympathy. Mussolini's rather theatrical pose as a 'protector of Islam' was the exception to this rule, but it remained futile.

The colonial nationalists either organised non-violent freedom movements or rose in sporadic rebellions which were readily suppressed by the colonial rulers. In their understandable anger, the colonial nationalists sometimes called their rulers fascists. Jawaharlal Nehru, in particular, who was influenced by European socialism and hated fascism, tried to see the system of colonial rule in a world context and stated that it was 'fascist'. In this, he was thinking more about the symptoms of repressive colonial rule than of the nature of fascism as a populist movement. But if one considers all repressive regimes defending a status quo as 'fascist' one does not contribute to an understanding of the true nature of fascism.

FASCISM IN EUROPE

Fascism in Europe did not owe its origin to the depression but had emerged after the First World War. The ruin of the old prewar world had left many people without orientation and with a strong quest for a new order. Fascism stressed national solidarity and posed as a protector of the nation against internal and external enemies. Thus the fascists could attract all those who felt that the old parties and the old political systems were thoroughly discredited and had to be replaced by something else. In a way these old parties paved the way for the fascists by behaving true to type and thus justifying prevalent prejudices. This happened in Italy earlier than in Germany. Mussolini had come to power long before the depression and had then mastered its impact by his dictatorial measures. He also challenged Great Britan and France by conquering Abyssinia and thus calling their bluff. In proving that the Western allies were helpless when confronted with this challenge, Mussolini encouraged Hitler's much more dangerous moves against them.

In contrast with socialism and communism, fascism did not

have a clearcut economic programme: its anti-communist stance was perhaps the only definite ideological position which the fascists could claim to have in this field. But there were some elements of corporatism and national autarky in fascist thought and this fitted in with the idea of a closed national economy as projected by Keynes. Of course, it could be argued that Keynes used the model of a closed economy only as an expository device and that he was not committed to this model in ideological terms. Nevertheless, there were elements of neo-mercantilism in his thought and he was attracted by the attention paid by the mercantilists to full employment. We do not wish to suggest here that Keynes influenced fascist economics. In fact, Hjalmar Schacht, Hitler's economic tsar before the war, had implemented quasi-Keynesian measures before Keynes published his *General Theory*. Our purpose in referring to Keynes in this context is only to show that it was the trend of the times to think along the lines developed by him. When asked about the backing of the Germany currency, Schacht had proclaimed boldly that the labour potential of the German people provided the backing for the German currency. This was economic populism – and it worked. The lack of an ideology wedded to explicit economic doctrines provided fascism with a great deal of flexibility in this field. Technocrats and financial wizards like Schacht had a free hand in Hitler's regime. They could prove their track record, and in this way bolster up a regime which was otherwise far removed from their own views and aspirations.

Fascism produced an atavistic regime. With its cult of the leader and its utter contempt for democracy it was more primitive and barbarian than the Italian and German monarchies of prewar times. On the other hand it was very modern in its use of the mass media and in its support of science and technology. It also crushed the 'distributional coalitions' (Olson 1982) of trade unions and industrialists which had stymied each other and had contributed to economic stagnation. All these organisations were 'switched' (*Gleichschaltung*) on to a common current. It is typical that a technical term was used for a political measure. In the short run this proved to be an excellent method of solving the problems created by the depression: social frictions were eliminated, wages were kept down, production stepped up and full employment was quickly achieved. But Hitler did not conceive of his regime merely as a means to overcome the depression, as Schacht did. Hitler had 'higher' aims and the technocratic problem solvers were only welcome as long as they helped to secure his regime.

To Hitler, the power which he had acquired in the 1930s was only a means to an end, and this end was global hegemony, 'switching' the whole world onto a common current. In this way fascism surpassed the vague populism of other problem solving dictators. This frightening vision which, however, fascinated his devoted followers, made all the difference. Generally populists were satisfied with limited measures of improvement, but the fascists talked of a 'revaluation of all values' (*Umwertung aller Werte*) and even intellectuals were attracted by this message. The recent debates concerning Heidegger's pronouncements at that time show some of the background of this attraction. There was a broad current of spiritual disillusionment in Germany after the First World War which went beyond the fact of physical defeat and the loss of some territories. People were looking for a new prophet and Hitler cashed in on that. Attempts have been made to interpret German intellectual history in such a way that fascism seems to emerge as the logical conclusion of the disappointments and aspirations of the time. This is certainly not true, but it would go beyond the scope of this book to discuss this in detail. Instead of going in for such 'teleological' explanations of the rise of fascism one should rather point to the rather eclectic and diffuse character of fascist 'ideology' which attracted all kinds of people – often for very different reasons. In this respect fascism shared many traits with other populist movements which also drew strength from diffuse sets of ideas rather than from intellectual clarity.

POPULISM IN LATIN AMERICA

In Latin America the impact of the depression gave rise to a quest for a national economic policy which would reduce dependence on the United States and on Europe. This quest was also directed against the indigenous oligarchies which were interested in their profits from exports and not in the development of the home market. These export-oriented oligarchies normally thought of themselves as 'liberals' and preached the doctrine of free trade, though they were not averse to deviating from these doctrines if they could benefit from subsidies or price stabilisation schemes. In order to get some political leverage, populist leaders could appeal to the lower classes which suffered from the impact of the depression. But whatever may be said about other Latin American countries, Argentina followed a different course in the years of the depression. This programme will be discussed first, before we return to the other countries.

Argentina had profited a great deal from the First World War: the war had restricted imports and at the same time given rise to some initial steps towards import substitution. There was a great deal of unrest and strikes in the postwar years, but in 1928 General Irigoyen once more came to power, and seemed to guarantee a return to prosperity, as he had ruled Argentina in the 'good years' of the war. Irigoyen represented the interests of the export-oriented agrarian oligarchy, the 'liberals' who were opposed to any interference with free trade. Accordingly he did nothing when the depression set in and was overthrown in 1930. But General Uriburu who replaced him, and his later successors, were by no means populists, they were conservative representatives of the same old agrarian oligarchy and were interested in maintaining good relations with Great Britain. The British were the main creditors and the best customers of Argentina. It was only after the Second World War that Argentina experienced a wave of populism, in this case Peronism, a kind of secondary reaction to the neglect of national interests during the years of the depression. Peron's most important social base was the urban workers and their trade unions. Looking back in anger at the 1930s, the Argentinians called that decade 'infamous' (*decada infama*) in which the British creditors in collusion with the agrarian oligarchy had prevented the rise of a national economic policy.

In Brazil the historical preconditions were somewhat different. There was also an export-oriented oligarchy claiming to be 'liberals', but since the price of their main export product, coffee, had been supported by state intervention, they had compromised their free trade convictions and were very much dependent on the government. This had exposed them to a great deal of criticism. There was an emerging industrial bourgeoisie in Brazil and a substantial urban working class. The depression upset earlier political equations. As we have seen in Chapter 10, Getulio Vargas emerged as a populist leader in this context and remained in power until 1945. He crushed a quasi-fascist movement, the Integralists, after feigning some sympathy with them for a while. He did cultivate good relations with fascist Germany, but he was

141

not a fascist himself. He sponsored a vague type of populism, but he never really headed a powerful movement of his own and rather preferred to divide and rule, balancing various interests and avoiding being too closely identified with any political group. In a way he preceded Peronism, but Peron was far more dependent on the trade unions than Vargas ever was.

A very vital populism which never quite made the grade was represented by the Apristas of Peru. The charismatic Victor Raul Haya de la Torre had founded the Alianza Popular Revolucionaria Americana in 1924. When the unpopular dictator Leguia was overthrown in 1930, the young Haya de la Torre could have emerged as a leader, rather like Vargas, but his party was banned from 1930 to 1957, and when he finally gained a majority of the votes in the presidential election of 1962, he nevertheless did not get the job. It was only in 1965 that his party could participate in forming a government in Peru. The problem for the Apristas was that Peru was subdivided into several rather isolated regional economies, but was ruled by a small oligarchy which always saw to it that the government remained in 'safe' hands. Under these circumstances the Apristas could not gain any stronghold or emerge as political brokers among various interests; they remained marginal to the political process, a permanent alternative, but with no chance of coming to power.

The Liberal Party of Columbia provides an example of successful populism. This party had a definite social programme which it tried to implement step by step. Unfortunately it came to a tragic end for this very reason. A noncommital and opportunistic approach might have saved it, but to the credit of its leaders it must be said that they had a vision and were not just interested in clinging to power for its own sake. The Liberals had been in opposition for forty-five years when the depression gave them a chance to defeat the conservative, export-oriented oligarchy in 1930. The first president did not make much of a mark, but his successor, Alfonso López Pumarejo, tried in earnest to implement the party programme by introducing land reforms and a progressive income tax. He also gave more power to the trades unions and changed the constitution so as to oblige the state to initiate a more equitable distribution of income. This was no mere populism, it was the comprehensive design of a development policy which would increase the purchasing power of the people, foster the home market and reduce the dependence on exports. The agrarian

142

oligarchy was naturally opposed to these reforms and the new industrial capitalists resented the imposition of taxes. The broadening of the social base of the Liberals was bitterly resented by the Conservative Party. A leading Liberal, Jorge Elicer Gaitan, who had piloted the land reforms introduced in 1934, was murdered by his political enemies in 1948. After this a bloody civil war erupted which ended with the imposition of military rule. This unfortunate example shows that a populist regime which came to power due to the depression could succumb to its conversative enemies once the economic situation had changed once more.

In this respect populism had a better fate in Mexico under President Lazaro Cardenas (1934–40). In Mexico the fights which beset attempts at reform had already taken place after the overthrow of the dictator, Porfirio Díaz, in 1911. Díaz was no populist, he was an old style law-and-order dictator. The revolutionary struggles after his overthrow had produced a new constitution by 1917 under which land reforms and the expropriation of foreign landlords had been achieved and oil and other natural resources had been declared national property, etc. Cardenas could go on from there, complete the land reforms, expropriate foreign oil companies and set up the state owned company Petroleos Mexicanos. He also reorganised his party and named it the Partido Revolucionario Institucional (Institutionalised Revolutionary Party), a strange name as it combined the otherwise contradictory ideas of revolution and institutionalisation. It was a clever piece of populist rhetoric as it suggested that the achievements of the revolution had now become properly institutionalised and thus preserved for all time to come. Cardenas had to face bitter opposition from the United States and Great Britain, but this certainly helped him to achieve national solidarity. While the depression years had led to this confrontation, the Second World War enabled Cardenas to get along with the United States once more. The United States was interested in good relations with its southern neighbour, the more so as millions of Mexican workers participated in the American war effort by working in various American industries.

It would be very interesting to review the fate of populism in other Latin American states, but this would go beyond the scope of this book. The other regimes would all fit into a scale marked by the conservative regime of Argentina in the '*decada infama*' at one end and Mexico's 'institutionalised revolution' at the other. A

143

similar scale can be constructed to encompass the various freedom movements against the colonial rulers in Africa and Asia.

THE COLONIAL FREEDOM MOVEMENTS

The scale of the colonial freedom movements reaches from quiet suffering in most parts of Africa to the victory of the Indian National Congress in the elections of 1937, based on the support of the newly enfranchised Indian peasantry. The political reaction to the depression depended on the previous development of the respective colonies. The intensity and duration of colonial rule and the growth of national organisations made all the difference. When the Indian National Congress was founded in 1885, colonialism in Africa was in its infancy. Even in the course of the twentieth century, colonial rule in Africa never achieved the degree of intensity which it had reached in India in the nineteenth century. Intensity refers not only to the colonial administration but also to the proliferation of law courts and colleges, etc. In India there were high courts and universities by the middle of the nineteenth century, there were Indian judges and, of course, innumerable Indian lawyers who then became the backbone of the freedom movement. By contrast we may mention the example of East Africa, where at the time when the respective colonies became independent states judges had to be imported from Ghana and Nigeria, because there was no qualified personnel available in East Africa. President Nyerere of Tanzania was the first man in his state who had gone abroad for higher education and returned with a university degree. If this was true of the 1960s one can imagine the absolute lack of leadership in the 1930s. There had also been hardly any attempts in Africa to introduce constitutional reforms and to enable the indigenous population to participate in any kind of political activity whatsoever.

In India constitutional reforms had already reached a relatively high level at the time of the depression, and another reform was just on the brink of adoption. The new reform promised provincial autonomy, i.e. the Indians were going to be permitted to form governments in the provinces of British India. In preparation for this reform a franchise commission had been set up, charged with the task of enfranchising at least 10 per cent of the population, especially the richer peasants who were supposed to be pro-British, as they had benefited from British tenancy legislation, etc.

144

The franchise was defined in terms of property qualifications and occupier tenancy was one of them. The British were convinced that the peasants had not been touched by the nationalism of the urban intelligentsia and would provide a solid social base for their rule. If the depression had not hit the peasants they probably would have remained loyal to the British, but the leadership of the Indian National Congress was well prepared by Mahatma Gandhi to listen to the grievances of the peasants and instead of the British it was the Congress which soon acquired a broad social base among the peasantry. In addition, the Congress leadership also gained the support of the peasants' enemies, the traders and money lenders, who also felt left in the lurch by the British. In trying to win the peasants the British colonial rulers had clamped down on the money lenders, but they lost the sympathies of both groups. The Congress leadership on the other hand could show concern for everybody's grievances and channel diverse types of discontent into the mainstream of nationalism. For the traders and money lenders it was of some importance that Gandhi also belonged to a caste of traders (*banias*). He had never stressed this, but he had sometimes referred to it jokingly when he collected funds for the Congress, indicating that he knew how to handle money and to keep accounts properly.

The special political situation in India has been discussed here in some detail in order to show how the convergence of the freedom movement with the unrest caused by the depression required numerous preconditions which were absent elsewhere. The example of Burma, which has been mentioned earlier (see Chapter 12), provides a study in contrasts. The Indian National Congress had never been active in Burma. It had condemned the British annexation of Upper Burma at its first session in 1885, but it had never shown any interests in the country after that. The educated elite of Burma was very tiny: the University of Rangoon had been established only in 1920. Posts in the colonial administration of Burma which were not reserved for the British were usually occupied by Indians, mostly Bengalis. The traders and money lenders in Burma were Chettiars from Southern India. No political organisation could have appealed at the same time to those outsiders and to Burmese peasants. The peasant uprising led by Saya San thus remained a sporadic event isolated from the mainstream of nationalism. After Saya San's execution in 1932 the Burmese peasants had no leader.

The small political elite of Burma was preoccupied with other matters at that time. The impending constitutional reform envisaged a separation of Burma from British India. This was not at all welcomed by the elite, because it was considered to be a British stratagem aimed at keeping Burma out of the mainstream of political progress. An Anti-Separation League was set up in 1932 in order to protest against this plan. This had nothing to do with the grievances of the Burmese peasants. A more radical course was adopted only in 1936 by a group of students at the University of Rangoon. Aung San, U Nu and Ne Win belonged to this group, which was known as the 'Thakins'. The students had added this honorific term to their names (*thakin* means gentleman) in order to challenge the superiority of the British Sahibs. They tried to combine nationalism and socialism in the same way as the Congress Socialist Party of India which had been established in 1934 by followers of Jawaharlal Nehru, although he never joined the party himself. The 'Thakins' were obviously influenced by the experience of the depression years. Thirty of them were later trained by the Japanese military in order to fight for Burmese independence with Japanese arms.

The Vietnamese freedom movement, which has also been mentioned before (see Chapter 12), could not get off the ground at all under the harshly repressive French colonial administration. The unrest of 1930 was suppressed very quickly. Ho Chi Minh, who later on emerged as the most prominent Vietnamese freedom fighter, could not even set foot on Vietnamese soil. He spent the decisive years from 1931–33 in a British jail in Hong Kong. He had already petitioned the victorious allies at their meeting in Versailles in 1919 for freedom and self-determination for his country, but at the time, nobody had listened to him. He had then turned to communism and worked as a Comintern agent in China. There he had tried to organise Vietnamese in exile. But his great moment came only after the war when he led the Vietnamese resistance against the returning French colonial rulers. Due to the policy of these rulers the national freedom movement of Vietnam remained a communist affair as no other political groups had had a chance to emerge under French rule. The harsh reaction of the French to the unrest of 1930 had set the pace for this kind of political development.

The Dutch in Indonesia were similar to the French in the harshness of their colonial rule. Here, too, it could easily have happened that the communists remained in charge of the national freedom movement, but the communists had already shown their hand in the 1920s and been brutally suppressed by the colonial administration. Thus only Sukarno's nationalist party, founded in 1927, was able to promote a freedom movement, although this party was also prosecuted and Sukarno spent the decisive years of the depression in jail. However, in 1930 he had contributed an important slogan to the incipient freedom movement: Marhaen. Later on Sukarno's populist ideology was actually called 'Marhaenism'. It was supposed to be a non-Marxist, radical socialism devoted to the uplift of the poor. Marhaen was the name of a peasant whom Sukarno had described as an example of the sufferings of the majority of the Indonesian people. Marhaen could not support his family with the rice grown on his field, and they lived below the poverty line. His sufferings were caused by the colonial rulers and he could be redeemed only by the freedom movement.

Sukarno's Marhaenism is a typical example of the populism of anti-colonial movements. Taking the fate of an individual as an illustration of the general conditions of the people corresponds to a figure of speech in classical Greek rhetoric which is called synecdoche, i.e. putting part for the whole. A further analysis of populist rhetoric would show that such figures of speech were used everywhere for conjuring up national solidarity. In addition to synecdoche there are metaphor and metonymy, the latter referring to a transfer of names. A typical example of a populist use of metonymy is Gandhi's use of the term *Harijan*(man of God) for the untouchables. A populist metaphor was Gandhi's term *Daridranarayan* (God is in the poor).

This use of rhetorical figures of speech went hand in hand with the increasing use of vernacular languages for the spread of political messages. The European political terminology derived from the languages of the colonial rulers had no meaning for the masses. Introducing such terms as loan words into the vernacular languages also did not help. The communists had particular problems with their Marxist terminology in this respect. A creative populist rhetoric which reflected the feelings of the masses was urgently needed. The depression accelerated this process of 'vernacularisation'. Before the shock of the depression the educated nationalists had conducted their political discourse in the language of their colonial rulers. As they had communicated, mostly, only among themselves, they got along very well in this manner. But when it came to addressing the peasants hit by the depression, they had to change their style. Some of them managed to create a new type of political discourse and also enriched the respective vernacular languages in this way.

The shock of the depression meant a change of consciousness for the people on the periphery of the world market. In Latin America this was caused by the clash between the people and the interests of the indigenous oligarchies and their foreign creditors; in Africa and Asia the harshness of colonial rule revealed by the reaction to the unrest caused by the depression induced such a change of mass consciousness. In keeping with the respective historical preconditions this resulted in immediate political consequences or in long term after effects which emerged only after the Second World War. Our review has highlighted some of the political consequences of the depression, but it is by no means comprehensive. More research along these lines would be most . rewarding.

15

FROM DEPRESSION TO WAR
Rearmament and economic growth

The depression was not the direct cause of the war, but there was at least one obvious link between it and the war: the rise of Hitler. The millions who voted for Hitler were deeply affected by the depression and believed in his promise to overcome it within a short time. Actually the depression receded very quickly under his rule, but this was only partly due to him – although he got the credit for it. But he was not satisfied with this achievement: his ambition was to start a war so as to conquer Europe and rule the world. There were enough hints at that in his published work, but it seems that nobody cared to read it. Moreover, in his first years in power he appeared to be rather cautious. His drive for rapid rearmament started only in 1936. This finally led to a rupture of his relations with Hjalmar Schacht whose brilliant economic policy had enabled Hitler to consolidate his power. Schacht was a conservative nationalist who worked for the revision of the conditions imposed upon Germany by the Treaty of Versailles. He supported Hitler to the extent that he fought for this aim, but he did not share his vision of global hegemony and opposed further expansionism once German power was restored within what he considered to be its legitimate limits. Thus the clash with Hitler was inevitable. In 1937 Schacht resigned from his post as minister of economic affairs and withdrew to the position of president of the Reichsbank. But in trying to protect Germany from inflation he was bound to clash with Hitler once more. Like Takahashi in Japan he had to be eliminated as he obstructed the drive for rearmament, but whereas Takahashi was murdered, Schacht only fell from grace and spent the rest of his life in relative obscurity.

ARMAMENT AND INFLATION: SCHACHT'S
CLASH WITH HITLER

In January 1939 Schacht wrote a courageous letter to Hitler which was also signed by the members of the board of the Reichsbank. He warned against the dangers of inflation. Full employment was nearly achieved and beyond that the printing of money and the increase of the national debt incurred for rearmament was bound to ruin the German economy. When Hitler received this letter he fired Schacht and the whole board of the Reichsbank. More money was printed and the national debt increased. Hitler was bent on preparing for a war and did not want to listen to economic reason. Schacht believed that all Hitler's aims were achieved by 1938 and the British thought so, too. Further armament could not be sustained economically in the long run, but Hitler was interested in conquest in the short run.

Schacht's warning against inflation was timely. From 1929 to 1932 the currency in circulation had diminished from 5.6 to 4.1 billion marks. Schacht had then cautiously reflated the currency by 300 million marks annually from 1933 to 1935 and by 500 million marks annually from 1935 to 1937. In 1937 the 1929 level had been surpassed. By then, 5.8 billion marks were in circulation and then there was a big jump to 8.6 billion in 1938. Once Schacht had been removed, the currency in circulation reached 12.7 billion marks in 1939. The increase in the national debt was even more alarming. It stood at 11.8 billion marks in 1933 and at 19 billion marks in 1937. At the end of 1938 it had risen to 30 billion marks, which is what caused Schacht to pull the alarm cord. Since this did not work and Hitler's train rushed ahead at full speed, the debt increased to 47.9 billion marks in 1939. German steel production is a good indicator of the rearmament drive. As the British and the French felt the need to do something about rearmament the prices of pig iron and steel in the world market had nearly doubled between 1936 and 1938. Nevertheless, German production grew at top speed and the British and French fell behind. Total steel production during the five years from 1935 to 1939 amounted to 102 million tonnes in Germany, 59 million tonnes in Great Britain and 35 million tonnes in France. In 1932 each of the three nations had produced only around 5 million tonnes of steel.

150

CONTRASTS: GERMANY AND THE WESTERN POWERS

Germany contrasted with Great Britain and France not only in terms of steel production: there were also important differences with regard to the levels of prices and wages. In Germany Hitler had eliminated the trades unions and his government controlled prices and wages. In Great Britain prices and wages rose substantially and France experienced an inflationary spurt of prices and wages after the devaluation of the franc in 1936. Table 15.1 shows these contrasts very vividly.

Table 15.1 Prices and wages: Germany, Britain and France (1929=100)

	Index of wholesale prices			Index of industrial wages		
	Germany	GB	France	Germany	GB	France
1932	70	75	65	67	96	104
1935	74	78	56	75	96	98
1936	76	83	65	78	99	115
1937	77	96	90	81	102	146
1938	77	89	103	85	105	161

A surge of production within a very short time brought about almost full employment in Germany. The index of industrial production (1937=100) stood at 48 in 1932 and at 110 in 1938. The respective figures for Great Britain were 68 and 97 and for France 91 and 92. Unemployment had not been a great problem for France: throughout the 1930s it never amounted to more than 3 per cent of the male workforce. Germany had 30 per cent unemployment in 1932 but only 2 per cent in 1938 whereas the respective index figures for Great Britain were 22 and 13.

The comparison of the three countries shows a lesser impact of the depression on Great Britain and France and a much stronger one on Germany. However, as far as recovery was concerned, Germany got out of the slump much faster than the other two countries, where the depression lingered on much longer. Neither Great Britain nor France were under great pressure to change their ways. The external pressure of Hitler's rise to power was at first neglected, then rearmament was stepped up in a half-hearted manner. This was enough to spur Hitler's drive to further rearmament but not enough to curb his ambitions.

Hitler had been aware of the weakness of Great Britain and France, but in contrast with his later years, when he was shown to be a maniac, he was rather diplomatic in the years from 1933 to 1935. He exploited the differences between the two powers: in 1935 he reached a naval agreement with the British which horrified the French. He then watched Mussolini's escapades in Abyssinia, and observed that neither the British nor the French reacted as they should have done. Thus Hitler felt encouraged to capture the occupied Rhineland, and when he got away with this, he went ahead with his plans. In a secret memorandum attached to his second Four Year Plan in 1936 he stated that the German army and the German economy must be ready for war within four years. Later on it appeared that his preparations for war were inadequate, but his successes in 1938, which were answered by a policy of appeasement, made him hope for a *Blitzkrieg* which would catch his rivals unprepared. The rapid capitulation of France convinced him even more. But in global perspective the 50 billion marks which he had invested in rearmament and the stock piling of material for the war by 1939 seemed to be a rather modest sum.

A GLOBAL IMPACT OF REARMAMENT?

The impact of rearmament on the world market remained rather limited. There was not much of a demand for imports as far as Germany and Japan – the two countries which invested most in rearmament – were concerned. Only such an increased demand could have had an effect on the world market. German imports increased only from 4.2 to 5.4 billion marks from 1933 to 1938 and German exports from 4.8 to 5.3 billion marks. Japanese foreign trade also did not increase at a very fast pace, as can be seen from Table 15.2.

Both Germany and Japan emphasised autarky and forced their respective populations to consume less and produce more. Japan tried hard to increase exports, whereas Germany relied heavily on bilateral barter trade agreements which by definition required a balanced arrangement. Japan, on the other hand, showed a rather asymmetrical relation with its two major trading partners, China and the United States. As Table 15.2 shows, Japanese exports to China and imports from the United States grew steadily. Japan's total balance of trade never showed a deficit, but with the United States there was a negative balance and with China a positive one.

Table 15.2 Japan's foreign trade (million yen)

	Total		With China		With USA	
	Import	Export	Import	Export	Import	Export
1932	1.9	1.8	0.2	0.3	0.5	0.4
1933	2.5	2.3	0.3	0.4	0.6	0.5
1934	3.0	2.8	0.3	0.6	0.8	0.4
1935	3.3	3.3	0.3	0.6	0.8	0.5
1936	3.6	3.6	0.4	0.7	0.8	0.6
1937	4.8	4.2	0.4	0.7	1.3	0.6
1938	3.8	3.9	0.6	1.2	0.9	0.4
1939	4.2	5.2	0.7	1.8	1.0	0.6
Total	27.1	27.1	3.2	6.3	6.7	4.0

It could be argued that Japan earned in China what it spent in the United States. Among the imports from the United States investment goods must have had a high priority and much of them must have served the armament industry. Japanese trade with China increased in spite of the Japanese attack on China: in fact Japanese exports to China doubled after 1937. Whether this was to the benefit of China may be doubted, although the theory of international trade tells us that trade must always be beneficial to the trading partners or else they would withdraw from it.

The increasing Japanese demand for American investment goods is perhaps one of the few contributions the drive for rearmament made to the revival of international trade. Of course, this did not help the periphery, which could only profit from a revival of the trade in raw materials. Japan and Germany mostly procured the raw materials they required from their particular zones of influence. Japan exploited Korea and Manchuria while Germany found in Southeastern Europe an area which could supply it with raw materials. At the most the rise in prices of iron and steel had a marginal impact on the world market. But the rise of these prices did not lead to an equivalent rise in other prices. The protectionism of closed national economies prevented a revival of international trade. Those states which were most intensively engaged in rearmament were also the most mercantilist ones.

The fact that rearmament did not have a very positive effect on the world market was revealed by the sudden recession which hit many countries in 1937–38 in the midst of the drive for the production of arms. Once more the Western industrialised countries were most immediately affected by this recession. In the United States, several factors contributed to it. One was the large sum spent on the veterans of the last war under an act passed in 1936. Roosevelt was opposed to it, but he could not stop it. The veterans received and spent about $1.4 billion in that year. This benefited the economy to the extent that it increased consumer spending, but it also reduced the ability of the federal government to opt for tax reductions or other measures. At the same time gold poured into the country and was sterilised because the United States had raised the amount required for their gold reserves. In the same year the reserve requirements of private banks were also increased, because it was feared that the bank credit might otherwise fuel another speculative boom. The fear of another crash dictated this policy, but combined with a rather tight fiscal policy this raising of reserve requirements had a contractionary effect which then contributed to a stock market crash instead of preventing it. The whole world had expected that the United States would lower the price of gold and this stimulated the de-hoarding of gold and its flow to the United States even more. People talked of an 'avalanche of gold' at that time, and traders hoarded raw materials and goods as they expected a rise in prices. Stock market speculation was rampant once more and it ended in another crash, in the autumn of 1937. Again there was a global fall in the prices of raw materials. Great Britain experienced a decline of production and a renewed increase of unemployment. To a somewhat lesser extent this was also true of France. Germany, which had isolated itself from the world market, was not affected by this recession.

The United States recovered fairly soon from this recession, but not due to expenditure on rearmament. Roosevelt, whose fiscal policy at the beginning of his second term had precipitated this depression, had quickly changed his course. His economic advisers had adopted Keynes' doctrine by now and did not mind incurring a budget deficit, although Roosevelt himself had always been against budget deficits. Even though the recession was short lived, it nevertheless affected the Western powers at a very awkward moment. In 1938 they had their last chance to stop Hitler, but instead of this they opted for appeasement. This policy should be assessed while keeping the economic context in mind.

The countries of the periphery felt the impact of this recession far more strongly. Almost none of them produced iron or steel, the only products whose prices increased during this recession. India, for instance, did export about 0.5 million tonnes of pig iron per year in the late 1930s and while it received only 12 million rupees for that volume of export in 1936 it got twice as much for it in subsequent years. However, agricultural prices were depressed once more, which was of greater importance for the majority of Indian people than the doubling of the price for pig iron.

It was only the outbreak of the war which relieved the countries of the periphery from the impact of the depression. Prices of agricultural produce and of raw materials rose steeply, but this created a different kind of problem. In India, for instance, the terrible Bengal famine caused the death of millions of people. It was entirely man made and had nothing to do with bad harvests. Speculators had cornered the market and the provincial government was unable and to some extent unwilling to check their activities. Clever operators made windfall gains during the war years, and the further redistribution of income from the poor to the rich which had begun in the years of the depression was greatly accelerated by the war.

16

THE AFTERMATH

Only thirty-one years separated the beginning of the First and the end of the Second World War. For Europe this was undoubtedly one of the worst periods of its history. The non-European periphery experienced this period in a different way: it did suffer from the depression, but for most countries of the periphery the wars meant chances for profit and economic growth. For the colonies the sequence war–depression–war ushered in the end of European colonial rule. Germany, which twice fought against the Western allies, made a decisive contribution to this process of the emancipation of the colonies. Of course, Germany did not go to war for this reason. On the contrary, it would have liked to retain or regain colonies itself. The loss of the German colonies after the First World War was for many Germans an additional reason to resent the Versaillés Treaty. Hitler was an admirer of British colonial rule and was certainly not interested in freeing African and Asian peoples from the yoke of colonialism. War aims and the consequences of war have rarely been compatible in history, and the consequences of the two world wars are an object lesson in this respect. The decolonialisation of the periphery and the rise of the United States to world hegemony were two unintended consequences of the process, which will be described in more detail in subsequent sections of this chapter.

The United States decided the outcome of both the First and the Second World War and in between it upset the world economic system instead of providing constructive leadership. This was not due to specific intentions but rather to the lack of a consistent policy. Even the entry into the Second World War was forced upon the United States, although it must be said that President Roosevelt was not at all reluctant to enter the war. He wanted to help the

Western allies, but could not take the initiative himself, because American public opinion was against joining the conflict. In the course of the war there emerged an American–British partnership which was not free from the rivalries that had already disturbed the cooperation between the two powers in the interwar period. We shall return to this issue when we discuss the rise of the United States. This has to be seen in the context of a third phenomenon, the decline of Europe due to two wars which could be called European civil wars, and to the depression which increased discord rather than cooperation.

THE EMANCIPATION OF THE COLONIAL PERIPHERY

'Pax Britannica', the unchallenged hegemony of Great Britain, was badly damaged by the First World War. All the colonial powers had benefited from this hegemony because it preserved the status quo, and the decline of Great Britain was therefore bound to damage the whole edifice of European colonial rule. The main pillar of the British empire was India, and for this reason India had a special role to play in the emancipation of the periphery. India had contributed substantially to the British war effort in the First World War, but it had also gained war profits. After the war an insecure Great Britain was confronted with a more self-confident India in which not only intellectuals but also traders and business-men harboured nationalist ideas and rallied around Mahatma Gandhi. British–Indian relations in the interwar period were marked by the fact that the British were neither willing nor able to suppress the Indian freedom movement by brute force. But they were also unwilling to grant Dominion status to India at a time when this would have been regarded as a generous concession. If India had been given that status in 1929 it would have been free to deal with the depression in its own way and would probably have entered the Second World War as a British ally. But under the impact of the depression Britain had to tighten its colonial control over India so as to avert its own bankruptcy.

When India got involved in the Second World War by supplying two million soldiers to the British, the colonial rulers were caught on the horns of a dilemma. The Atlantic Charter which they had signed with their American allies promised freedom and self-determination to all peoples of the world. They had also concluded an agreement with the Americans which was designed to prevent the accumulation of war debts which had beset American–British relations after the First World War. The agreement stipulated that all nations participating in the war effort should share the burden equitably. But Churchill had made it clear that the Atlantic Charter would not apply to India and other colonies. Since India thus was not a free ally it could not be forced to share the financial burden of the war effort and all its contributions had to be credited to its account with the Bank of England. This indebtedness to India was mentioned by the British to the Americans whenever they wanted to cut American aid because they noticed that dollar reserves were accumulating in London. Churchill was furious about the British war debt to India and would have liked to cancel it by defining it as India's contribution to the allied war effort. However, the Americans were watching him and he could not have it both ways. In India a British cancellation of these war debts would also have caused alarm and led to a reduction of Indian deliveries. After all, Indian private industry supplied the British with essential goods and a cancellation of debts would have ruined British credit-worthiness. Leopold Amery, the secretary of state for India, told Churchill that it would be unwise to tell a taxi driver on an urgent trip that one would not pay for it at the end of the journey. Amery had an over-optimistic idea of the postwar use of Indian balances in the Bank of England, believing that they would help to boost British exports. This led Keynes to describe him as a dangerous lunatic. Keynes had a different view of what Amery considered to be a potentially positive effect. To him this potential Indian claim on British goods amounted to a mortgage on British postwar production. But neither Churchill nor Keynes could prevent the accumulation of Indian balances in the Bank of England, which finally contributed to India's independence.

The other colonies neither had as much share in the war effort as India, nor did they have the institutional infrastructure for a smooth transfer of power. But once the main pillar of the British empire had been removed, the rest of the edifice was bound to crumble sooner or later. The African colonies had not supplied the allies with anything useful for the war effort. All they had to offer was agricultural produce of a non-essential kind which could be dispensed with in war time. Instead of profiting from these African colonies the British had to try hard to find some use for their products so as not to let them slide into another depression.

Therefore they established marketing boards which were mostly run by the old trading companies and permitted them to make some profit even during the war. In the colonies where white settlers predominated, they managed to control these marketing boards and used them to their own benefit. After the Americans had entered the war, the British tried to involve them in their colonial system so as to prevent them from becoming competitors. However, the Americans had their own aims in this respect: they did not want to perpetuate old fashioned colonialism but were interested in an open door policy. This economic policy, rather than an altruistic interest in the Atlantic Charter, was at the bottom of American anti-colonialism. But as this policy and the defence of the Atlantic Charter did not contradict each other, it was possible to pursue them both at the same time.

The smaller European colonial powers, the French, the Dutch and the Portuguese, did not have problems identical with those the British had to face, but they obviously could not hope to perpetuate their colonial rule for ever once British rule had disappeared. The French colonies had also been hit very hard by the depression. After Hitler's occupation of France, the French colonies were governed by agents of the Vichy regime or by the Free French of General de Gaulle. Some French colonies were taken over by the British or the Americans. In Indochina the French were replaced by the Japanese who also took over Indonesia from the Dutch. The return of the earlier colonial powers to Indochina and Indonesia after the war constitutes one of the worst chapters of colonial history. The Portuguese, the oldest allies of the British, had maintained their colonial empire in the shadow of the British one. Their neutrality in the Second World War helped them to hold on to their colonial possessions without any interference, but their days as colonial rulers were also numbered.

In discussing the end of colonialism we should recall that the general deterioration of the terms of trade for the periphery had reduced the value of colonies. The cost of their administration increased while the profits which could be derived from them declined. It would have been very profitable to have had the West Asian oil producing countries under colonial rule in the years after 1973, but all other colonies would have been a liability rather than an asset. Moreover, any attempt at dominating such places was bound to land the power concerned in an international mess as the case of Indochina clearly shows.

THE RISE OF THE UNITED STATES

It was an irony of fate that the United States got involved in Indochina, whose path to emancipation from colonial rule had been beset by the greatest difficulties. If the Americans had insisted on the implementation of the intentions of the Atlantic Charter immediately after the war, they might have avoided this very messy affair – but the Vietnam War is far beyond the period with which we are concerned here. We shall return instead to the origins of the rise of the United States which proved to be a very reluctant hegemonic power to begin with.

The entry of the United States into the First World War was a much delayed initiative which was finally provoked by the German intensification of submarine warfare. The Americans had invested a great deal of money in the European war effort even before they entered the hostilities. Due to this, the relation of debtor and creditor had been reversed. Before the war the United States had owed $4 billion to the European powers, but in the course of the war their erstwhile creditors became debtors and by the end of the war the European allies owed $11 billion to the United States. President Wilson's idealistic rhetoric, which even at that time reflected the American dream of 'making the world safe for democracy', camouflaged the practical necessity for the Americans to save their European debtors if they wanted their debts to be repaid. This does not mean that Wilson did not believe in what he said. He was definitely interested in establishing a peaceful world order after the war. Unfortunately, he did not use his political clout to good effect and was not taken seriously by his European allies, who could not have won the war without his help. He did not make the slightest attempt to use his position as a creditor to put the European powers under pressure. There was a good reason for this: the Americans regarded the war debts of their allies before and after the conclusion of the Versailles Treaty as something quite separate from the political problems at stake. If they had wished to make political use of their position as a creditor nation they would have also had to make financial concessions in order to 'buy' political concessions from the allies. This the European powers would have understood and a comprehensive bargain could have emerged which would have given the Americans a much more important role in postwar Europe. But to the European politicians the Americans appeared to be both loquacious apostles of peace and deaf-mute creditors.

The return of the United States to the principles of isolationism was a blow to the prospects of a new world order. The loquacious apostle of peace turned his back on Europe, but the deaf-mute creditor stayed on. At the same time the European powers harboured the illusion that they could preserve the order embodied in the Versailles Treaty without American support and interference. That they were unable to maintain this order in a constructive way was shown by their inability to settle the problem of German reparations. Here again the Americans had to act as mediators (the Dawes Plan, the Young Plan). Once more, however, the Americans failed to derive political capital from their position as creditors. In fact, the booming American business of exporting capital to Europe and especially to Germany was strictly kept apart from all political considerations.

When the depression hit the world, the Americans added economic isolation to their political isolationist stance. They did nothing to get Europe out of the financial mess which was to a large extent due to their own financial behaviour. At the same time they enshrined their political isolationism in a law obliging them to observe neutrality in any future war. Thereby they gave a clear signal to those who wished to challenge the order established at Versailles that they could do so without having to fear American intervention. However, the Americans did consolidate their own economic position in the meantime and when they finally had to enter a war once more, they were in a position to mobilise millions of soldiers and produce an enormous number of ships and plenty of armaments. Moreover, by means of the Lend–Lease Act passed on 11 March 1940 they provided credit to their allies to the tune of $60 billion. But the actual American entry into the war again required a provocation – this time by the Japanese who attacked Pearl Harbor on 7 December 1941.

Basically the Second World War then proceeded along the same lines as the first one, except there was more widespread suffering this time and the fight to the finish took longer than in the First World War. After the war the Americans could have withdrawn from Europe once more, but this time there was nobody around who would have dared to claim the ability to restore order without American help. France was completely down and out, Great Britain was exhausted from the war effort. But this time there was also the Soviet Union and it was obvious that the United States did not want to leave Europe to this new power. In a way one could say that it was due to the Soviet Union that the Americans stayed on this time. Of course, this also meant the beginning of the Cold War, which converted Europe into an arena for the power struggle of the two new giants.

THE DECLINE OF EUROPE

The rapid decline of Europe from the eminent position in the world which it held in 1914 to the misery of 1945 was brought about by the sequence war–depression–war. The two wars were, in effect, European civil wars which were due to the German problem. There have been futile controversies about the German quest for world power in 1914. While some historians have documented the German will to power in detail others have argued that in economic terms Germany was not at all prepared for war and thus it would be nonsense to talk of such a quest for power. But this does not settle the issue, as one may very well pursue an aim even if one is ill equipped for its achievement. It is also futile to attribute too much to the martial rhetoric of Emperor Wilhelm II. Quotations from his speeches provided excellent material for Allied war propaganda later on, but the real problem of the prewar German political system was that an emperor could make such irresponsible speeches without any kind of control.

The prewar German political system was antediluvian when compared to the British or French systems. Its archaic structure was out of step with the enormous economic and scientific progress made by Germany in the late nineteenth century. In addition there was the connection between the archaic German state and the equally archaic Austro–Hungarian monarchy. It was extremely difficult to find a common denominator between these archaic regimes and the Western European nation states. The latter finally adopted a policy of 'containment' which made the Germans feel that they were under a state of siege. When war broke out, it was a conflict which nobody actually wanted but everybody concerned had prepared for.

As has been amply demonstrated in the previous chapter, postwar cooperation among the allies was sadly lacking. Their political solidarity was weak and was further undermined by the depression and by their inability to organise international economic cooperation. The failure of the World Economic Conference of 1933 showed this very clearly. In the same year Hitler came to power in Germany and soon began to pursue the aggressive policy which ushered in another war. He wanted to crush Europe and reorganise it under his command and he received no signals that he would not be permitted to do so. He did ruin Europe, and it was only rescued by America. In contrast to its ambiguous role in the interwar period, Germany emerged after the war as America's most obedient ally and at the same time as an advocate of the political and economic integration of Europe.

The bitter experience of the sequence of war–depression–war seems to have contributed to a new awareness of the need for European cooperation in a world which is no longer dominated by Europe, but in which it has to play an important role. In the interwar period this had not yet dawned upon European leaders.

BIBLIOGRAPHICAL NOTES

Abbreviations

NPE=Eatwell, J. *et al.* (eds) *The New Palgrave. A Dictionary of Economics*, 4 vols, London: Macmillan 1987.

NPM=Newman, P. *et al.* (eds) *The New Palgrave Dictionary of Money and Finance*, 3 vols, London: Macmillan 1992.

1 INTRODUCTION: ECONOMICS AND THE DEPRESSION

The depression as a challenge to economic doctrine

Peter Temin, *Did monetary forces cause the Great Depression?*, New York: Norton 1976; Peter Temin, *Lessons from the Great Depression*, Cambridge, Mass.: MIT Press 1989; Charles P. Kindleberger, *The World in Depression, 1929–1939*, Berkeley: University of California Press 1986 (2nd edn). For a survey of the attempts at fitting the Great Depression into the pattern of business cycles see S. Pollard, 'Depressions', in NPE, Vol. 1, p. 809 ff.; on monetarism see P. Cagan, 'Monetarism', in NPM, Vol.1, p. 719 ff.; for a review of the impact of the depression on various countries see Hermann van der Wee (ed.) *The Great Depression Revisited*, The Hague: Nijhoff 1972; for monetarist interpretations of the depression see Karl Brunner (ed.) *The Great Depression Revisited*, Boston/ The Hague: Kluwer-Nijhoff 1981.

Keynes and the theory of economic disequilibrium

John Maynard Keynes, *The General Theory of Employment, Interest and Money*, (The Collected Works of J. M. Keynes, Vol. VII) London: Macmillan 1973; Hyman Minsky, *John Maynard Keynes*, New York: Columbia University Press 1975; Peter Clarke, *The Keynesian Revolution in the Making, 1924-1936*, Oxford: Clarendon Press 1988; Roger Middleton, *Towards the Managed Economy: Keynes, the Treasury and the fiscal policy debate of the 1930s,*

London: Methuen 1985; see also the articles 'Keynes' (D. Patinkin),'Keynes's General Theory' (M. Milgate), 'Keynesianism' (J. Eatwell), 'Keynesian Revolution' (L.Tarshis), in NPE, Vol. 3; Walter Allan (ed.) *A Critique of Keynesian Economics*, London: Macmillan 1993.

Neo-mercantilism or 'Beggar-thy-neighbour'

For a detailed discussion of competitive devaluation in various countries see the contributions to *Weltwirtschaftliches Archiv*, 43/1 (January 1936). It contains articles by N. F. Hall (on Great Britain), E. Lindahl (on Sweden), C. W. G. Schumann (on South Africa). K. Matsuoka (on Japan), H. Max (on Chile) and J. Donaldson (on the USA); for the term 'beggar-thy-neighbour' see the respective article in NPE, Vol 1, p. 220 (Nilufer Cagatay); see also the article 'Joan Robinson', in NPE, Vol. 4, p. 212 (L. Pasinetti).

A blind spot: the fate of the periphery

Some of the reasons for the blindness of economists in this respect are mentioned in passing by Charles Kindleberger in his contribution to the volume edited by Rosemary Thorp (see notes to Chapter 10). For Fisher's 'debt–deflation' theory see the article 'Irving Fisher' (J. Tobin) in NPE, Vol. 2, p. 375.

The web of credit

For the process of 'interlinking' credit transactions see the article 'Credit markets in developing countries' (C. Bell), in NPM, Vol.1. The evidence given by Benjamin Strong to the House of Representatives is discussed by David C. Wheelock, 'Monetary Policy in the Great Depression: What the Fed did, and Why', in *The Federal Reserve Bank of St Louis Review*, March/April 1992 pp. 3–28. Wheelock also provides a detailed analysis of Federal Reserve credit. For customary law in the colonies and the patterns of taxation see J. de Moor and D. Rothermund (eds)*Our Laws, Their Lands. Land laws and land use in modern colonial societies*, Münster: Lit 1994.

2 THE TRAGEDY OF THE INTERNATIONAL GOLD STANDARD

The Bank of England and the gold standard

Barry Eichengreen, *Golden Fetters: the gold standard and the Great Depression*, New York: Oxford University Press 1992; R. S. Sayers, *The Bank of England, 1891–1944*, 3 vols, Cambridge: Cambridge University Press 1976; A.I. Bloomfield, *Monetary Policy under the International Gold Standard, 1880–1914*, New York: Federal Reserve Bank of New York 1959; Marcello de Cecco, *The International Gold Standard: Money and Empire*, London: Frances

Pinter 1984 (2nd edn); see also the article 'Gold standard' (M. de Cecco), in NPE, Vol. 2, pp. 539–44; Hansjörg Herr, 'Der Goldstandard und die währungspolitische Diskussion in der Klassik', in *Konjunkturpolitik*, 34/1 1988, Berlin: Duncker & Humblot.

The defeat of bimetallism

See the article 'Bimetallism' (M. D. Bordo), in NPM, Vol. 1, pp. 208–10; for India see D. Rothermund, 'India's Silver Currency. An Aspect of the Monetary Policy of British Imperialism', in *Indian Economic and Social History Review*, 7 (1970), pp. 351–67.

The return to the gold standard

Diane B. Kunz, *The Battle for Britain's Gold Standard in 1931*, London: Croom Helm 1987; Donald E. Moggridge, *British Monetary Policy 1924 – 1931: The Norman Conquest of $4.86*, Cambridge: Cambridge University Press 1972; for the return of other nations to the gold standard see Eichengreen, op.cit. pp. 187–210.

The instruments of monetary policy

For further explanations of these instruments see the following articles in NPM: 'Bank rate', Vol. 1, p. 170 (S. Howson), 'Open-market operations', Vol. 3, p. 74 (S.H. Axilrod and H.C. Wallich), and 'Reserve requirements', Vol. 3, p. 343 (M.E. Sushka).

3 THE DILEMMA OF WAR DEBTS AND REPARATIONS

The dimensions of war debts and reparations

See the article 'Reparations' in NPE, Vol. 4, p. 149 (I. Drummond); see also William C. McNeil, *American Money in the Weimar Republic. Economics and Politics at the Eve of the Great Depression*, New York: Columbia University Press 1986.

The Dawes Plan; a precarious solution to the dilemma

Parker Gilbert's activities and the Dawes Plan are discussed by W. McNeil, op.cit.; see also S.A. Schuker, *The End of French Predominance in Europe: The Financial Crisis of 1924 and the Dawes Plan*, Chapel Hill: University of North Carolina Press 1976.

The pattern of political rivalries

Frank B. Tipton and Robert Aldrich, *An Economic and Social History of Europe, 1890–1939*, London: Macmillan 1987; Paul Kennedy, *The Rise and Fall of Great Empires. Economic Change and Military Conflict from 1500 to 2000*, New York: Random House 1987.

4 WORLD PRODUCTION OF AGRICULTURAL PRODUCE

Wheat production

Ingmar Svennilson, *Growth and Stagnation in the European Economy*, Geneva: United Nations Economic Commission for Europe 1954; V.P. Timoshenkov, *World Agriculture in the Great Depression*, Ann Arbor: Michigan Business Studies Vol. 5, 1933.

Asian rice production

For data on the world rice production (except China) see A.J.H. Latham, *The Depression and the Developing World, 1915–1939*, London: Croom Helm 1981.

Scenarios A and B

Output and prices of the commodities mentioned here are discussed by C. Kindleberger op.cit.; for tea see D. Rothermund, *India in the Great Depression, 1929–1939*, New Delhi: Manohar 1992.

5 THE ORIGIN OF THE DEPRESSION IN AMERICA

Income distribution, the concentration of capital and the lack of investment

Thomas C. Cochran, *The American Business System*, Cambridge, Mass.: Harvard University Press 1957; P. Fearon, 'Hoover, Roosevelt and American economic policy during the 1930s', in W. R. Garside (ed.) *Capitalism in Crisis. International Responses to the Great Depression*, London: Frances Pinter, 1993, pp. 114–47; for a survey of the literature on the depression in America see ABC-Clio Information Services, *The Great Depression. A historical bibliography*, Santa Barbara: ABC-Clio Inc. 1984. The figures concerning cars and trucks are from the 'Report of the Committee on Recent Economic Changes of the President's Conference on Unemployment (Chairman: Herbert Hoover)', New York: 1929.

Financial intermediation: bankers and speculators

See the books by Kindleberger and Temin mentioned above in notes to Chapter 1; Milton Friedmann and Anna J. Schwartz, *A Monetary History of the United States, 1867–1960*, Princeton: Princeton University Press 1963; David C. Wheelock, 'Monetary Policy in the Great Depression: What the Fed. Did, and Why', in *The Federal Reserve Bank of St Louis Review*, 2 (1992) pp. 3–27; Lauchlin Currie, *The Supply and Control of Money in the United States* (Harvard Economic Studies Vol. 47), Cambridge, Mass.: Harvard University Press 1934.

The external economic relations of the United States

Detlef Junker, *Der unteilbare Weltmarkt. Das ökonomische Interesse in der Außenpolitik der USA, 1933–1941*, Stuttgart: Klett 1975; see also C. Kindleberger, op.cit., on the Smoot/ Hawley Act and the Hoover Moratorium.

Roosevelt's domestic and foreign economic policy

For the argument concerning Roosevelt's 'new regime' see Peter Temin, op.cit. (1989); for putting the blame on Roosevelt with regard to the wrecking of the World Economic Conference see Charles Kindleberger, op.cit.; for a close-up of Roosevelt's actions see Barry Eichengreen, op. cit.; see also Margaret Weir and Theda Skocpol, 'State Structures and Possibilities for "Keynesian" Responses to the Great Depression in Sweden, Britain, and the United States', in Peter B. Evans *et al.* (eds) *Bringing the State Back In*, Cambridge: Cambridge University Press 1985, pp.107–68. The authors discuss the problems of a weak federal government, the new monetary policy of the Federal Reserve Board under Marriner Eccles and his assistant Lauchlin Currie, and the role of the Harvard group of Keynesian economists in the late 1930s.

6 THE TRANSMISSION OF THE CRISIS TO EUROPE

Great Britain

Alan Booth and Melvyn Pack, *Employment, Capital and Economic Policy. Great Britain 1918–1939*, Oxford: Blackwell 1985; Nigel Gray, *The Worst of Times. An oral history of the Great Depression in Britain*, London: Wildwood House 1985; Alan Booth, 'The British reaction to the economic crisis', in W. Garside (ed.) op. cit., pp. 30–55; Geoffrey Jones, *British Multinational Banking, 1830–1990*, Oxford: Clarendon Press 1993; Forrest Capie, *Depression and Protectionism. Britain between the wars*, London: George Allen & Unwin 1983; Ian Drummond, *The Floating Pound and the Sterling Area*,

1931–1939, Cambridge: Cambridge University Press 1981; Forrest Capie *et al.*, 'What happened in 1931?' in Forrest Capie and Geoffrey E. Wood (eds) *Financial Crises and the World Banking System,* London: Macmillan 1986, pp. 122–59; Susan Howson and Donald Winch, *The Economic Advisory Council. A Study in Economic Advice during Depression and Recovery,*Cambridge: Cambridge University Press 1977; Steven Tolliday, *Business, Banking and Politics. The Case of British Steel, 1918–1939,* Cambridge, Mass.: Harvard University Press 1987.

Germany

Harold James, *The German Slump. Politics and Economics, 1924–1936,* Oxford: Clarendon Press 1986; Harold James, 'Innovation and conservatism in economic recovery. The alleged "Nazi recovery" of the 1930s', in W.R. Garside (ed.) op. cit., pp. 70–95; Edward W. Bennett, *Germany and the Financial Crisis 1931,* Cambridge Mass.: Harvard University Press 1962; Knut Borchardt, *Wachstum, Krisen, Handlungsspielräume der Wirtschaftspolitik,* Göttingen: Vandenhoek 1982; K. Borchardt and H. O. Schötz (eds) *Wirtschaftspolitik in der Krise. Die (Geheim)Konferenz der Friedrich-List-Gesellschaft über Möglichkeiten und Folgen einer Kreditausweitung,* Baden-Baden: Nomos 1991; Verena Schröter, *Die deutsche Industrie auf dem Weltmarkt 1929 bis 1933. Außenwirtschaftliche Strategien auf dem Weltmarkt,* Frankfurt: Peter Lang 1984; for an analysis of 'distributional coalitions' see Mancur Olson, *The Rise and Decline of Nations,* New Haven: Yale University Press 1982.

France

Julian Jackson, *The Politics of Depression in France, 1932–1936,* Cambridge: Cambridge University Press 1985; L.D. Schwartz, 'Searching for recovery: unbalanced budgets, deflation and rearmament in France during the 1930s', in W.R. Garside (ed.) op. cit., pp. 96–113; James F. McMillan, *Twentieth Century France. Politics and Society 1898–1991,* London: Edward Arnold 1992.

Sweden

Lars Jonung, 'The Depression in Sweden and in the United States. A Comparison of Causes and Policies', in Karl Brunner (ed.) op.cit., pp. 286–315; B. Gustafsson, 'Unemployment and fiscal policy in Sweden', in W.R. Garside, op. cit., pp. 56–69; see also M. Weir and T. Skocpol, op.cit., pp. 107–68 on the successful coalition of social democrats and farmers in Sweden. I am grateful to my former student Peter Schlesier for an excellent seminar paper on 'Die Voraussetzungen für ein erfolgreiches Krisenmanagement in Schweden'.

This chapter is based on the book by Camilla Dawletschin-Linder, *Die Türkei und Ägypten in der Weltwirtschaftskrise, 1929–1933,* Stuttgart: Steiner 1989. I am grateful to Dr Dawletschin-Linder for answering my questions and for reading the first draft of this chapter; see also Roger Owen, 'Egypt in the World Depression: Agricultural Recession and Industrial Expansion', in Ian Brown (ed.) *The Economies of Africa and Asia in the Inter-war Depression,* London: Routledge 1989, pp. 137–51.

8 AUSTRALIA'S REACTION: OVERPRODUCTION AND DEVALUATION

This chapter is based on the book by C.B. Schedvin, *Australia and the Great Depression,* Sydney: Sydney University Press 1970. Reprint 1988; see also A.M. Endres and K.E. Jackson, 'Policy responses to the crisis: Australasia in the 1930s', in W.R. Garside (ed.) op. cit., pp. 148–65.

9 COLONIAL CRISIS MANAGEMENT: THE CASE OF INDIA

This chapter is based on the research monograph: D. Rothermund, *India in the Great Depression, 1929–1939,* New Delhi: Manohar 1992.

10 THE NEW ROLE OF THE STATE IN LATIN AMERICA

For a general assessment of devaluations and defaults on international debts of the Latin American states in the depression see Albert Fishlow, 'Hard Times: Latin America in the 1930s and 1980s', in Carl-Ludwig Holtfrerich (ed.) *Interactions in the World Economy. Perspectives from International Economic History,* New York: Harvester Wheatsheaf 1989. For a critical review of the emphasis on industrial import substitution see Victor Bulmer-Thomas, *The Economic History of Latin America since Independence,* Cambridge: Cambridge University Press 1994, pp. 223–37

'Reactive' and 'passive' states

C. F. Díaz Alejandro, 'Latin America in the 1930s', in Rosemary Thorp (ed.) *Latin America in the 1930s. The Role of the Periphery in World Crisis,* London: Macmillan 1984, pp. 17–49.

BIBLIOGRAPHICAL NOTES

Brazil and Colombia

Marcelo de Paiva Abreu, 'Argentina and Brazil during the 1930s: The Impact of British and American International Economic Policies', in R.Thorp (ed.) op.cit., pp. 144–62; I am grateful to Dr Jens Hentschke for letting me read the manuscript of his unpublished work on the 'Estado Novo' in Brazil and for reading the passage on Brazil in this chapter. His suggestions have helped me a great deal; José Antonio Ocampo, 'The Colombian Economy in the 1930s', in R.Thorp (ed.) op cit., pp. 117–43; Hans-Joachim König, 'Latinamerika in der Krise: Das Beispiel Kolumbien', in D. Rothermund (ed.) *Die Peripherie in der Krise: Afrika, Asien, Lateinamerika,* Paderborn: Schöningh 1982, pp. 245–84.

Chile and Peru

Gabriel Palma, 'From an Export-led to an Import-substituting Economy: Chile 1914–1939', in R.Thorp (ed.) op.cit., pp. 50–80; R.Thorp and Carlos Londono, 'The Effect of the Great Depression on the Economies of Peru and Colombia', in R.Thorp (ed.) op cit., pp. 81–116.

Argentina and Mexico

Arturo O'Connell, 'Argentina into the Depression: Problems of an Open Economy', in R. Thorp (ed.) op. cit., pp. 118–221; Enrique Cardenas, 'The Great Depression and Industrialisation: The Case of Mexico', in R. Thorp (ed.) op.cit., pp. 222–41; E.V.K. FitzGerald, 'Restructuring through the Depression: The State and Capital Accumulation in Mexico, 1925–1940', in R. Thorp (ed.) op. cit., pp. 242–65.

11 CONTRASTS IN EAST ASIA: CHINA AND JAPAN

The delayed emergence of the crisis in China

Albert Feuerwerker, *The Chinese Economy, 1912–1949,* Ann Arbor: University of Michigan Press 1968; the Chinese currency problems of this period are discussed by Liao Bao-seing, *Die Bedeutung des Silberproblems für die chinesischen Währungsverhältnisse,* Berlin: Duncker & Humbolt 1939; on Chinese rice prices and silver see Yeh-Chieng Wang, 'Secular Trends in Rice Prices in the Yangzi Delta, 1638– 1935', in Thomas G. Rawski and Lillian M. Li (eds) *Chinese History in Economic Perspective,* Berkeley: University of California Press 1992, pp. 35–68; on land and income see Loren Brandt and Barbara Sands, 'Land Concentration and Income Distribution in Republican China', in T. G. Rawski and L. M. Li (eds) op.cit., pp. 179–206; for the 'revisionist' interpretation see Ramon H.

171

Myers, 'The World Depression and the Chinese Economy', in Ian Brown (ed.) op.cit., pp. 253–78.

Crisis management in Japan

G. C. Allen, *A Short Economic History of Modern Japan*, London: Macmillan 1983 (4th edn); for a blow-by-blow account of the depreciation of the yen see Takatoshi Ito *et al.*, 'News and the Dollar/Yen Exchange Rate 1931–1933: The End of the Gold Standard, Imperialism and the Great Depression' in *Journal of Japanese and International Economics* 7 (1993), pp. 107–31. The authors show that the immediate depreciation of about 30 per cent at the end of 1931 was expected and intended; the further radical depreciation in the course of 1932 was not intended by the government and was even resented by Japanese industry; it was caused by reactions abroad to Japanese military adventurism; see also Kaoru Sugihara, 'Japan's Industrial Recovery, 1931–1936', in Ian Brown (ed.) op.cit. pp. 152–69; for the sufferings of the rural people see Ann Waswo, 'Japan's Rural Economy in Crisis', in Ian Brown (ed.) op.cit., pp. 115–36.

12 REACTIONS TO THE DEPRESSION IN SOUTHEAST ASIA

Java and the Philippines: contrasting patterns of sugar export

Peter Boomgard, 'Treacherous Cane: The Java Sugar Industry between 1914 and 1940' in Bill Albert and Adrian Graves (eds)*The World Sugar Industry in War and Depression*, London: Routledge 1988, pp. 157–69; Clifford Geertz, *Agricultural Involution. The Process of Ecological Change in Indonesia*, Berkeley: University of California Press 1963; Yoshiko Nagano, 'The Oligopolistic Structure of the Philippine Sugar Industry during the Depression', in B. Albert and A. Graves (eds) op.cit., pp. 170–81; Norman G. Owen, 'Subsistence in the Slump: Agricultural Subsistence in the Provincial Philippines' in Ian Brown (ed.) op.cit., pp. 94–114.

The crisis of the rice export economy of Burma

Micheal Adas, *The Burma Delta: Economic Development and Social Change on an Asian Rice Frontier, 1852–1941*, Madison: University of Wisconsin Press 1974; James Scott,*The Moral Economy of the Peasant: Rebellion and Subsistence in Southeast Asia*. New Haven: Yale University Press 1976. The author discusses the rebellion led by Saya San in the context of the concept of 'moral economy', but does not link it with the compulsion of the credit system and the impending fall of the rice price caused by the price fall in Japan.

Peasant resistance in Vietnam

James Scott, op.cit, contains a detailed account of the peasant rebellions; see also Pierre Brocheux, 'Crise économique et société en Indochine francaise', in Catharine Coquery-Vidrovitch (ed.) *L'Afrique et la crise de 1930*. Numéro spécial, Revue francaise d'outre mer, Vol.63, Paris: Presses Universitaires 1976.

13 THE FATE OF AFRICA

For a survey of colonial land legislation see Jaap de Moor and Dietmar Rothermund (eds) *Our Laws, Their Lands. Land use and land laws in modern colonial societies*, Münster: Lit Verlag 1995.

Currencies and competition

The volume edited by C. Coquery-Vidrovitch op.cit., contains several contributions which document the disadvantages due to French adherence to the gold standard.

West Africa: African producers and European traders

Helmut Bley 'Die koloniale Dauerkrise in Westafrika. Das Beispiel Nigeria', in D. Rothermund (ed.) op.cit., pp. 37–58; S.M. Martin, 'The Long Depression: West African Export Producers and the World Economy, 1914–1945', in Ian Brown op.cit., pp. 74–94. See also Katja Füllberg-Stolberg, *Nordnigeria während der Wirtschaftskrise, 1929–1939*, unpublished PhD thesis, University of Hanover 1989; Axel Harneit-Sievers, *Zwischen Depression und Dekolonisation: Afrikanische Händler und Politik in Südnigeria, 1935–1954*, Saarbrücken: Breitenbach 1991.

The command economy of the Belgian Congo

Albert Wirz, 'Die Entwicklung der kolonialen Zwangswirtschaft in Belgisch-Kongo', in D. Rothermund (ed.) op.cit., pp. 59–80; B. Jewsiewicki, 'The Great Depression and the making of the colonial economic system in the Belgian Congo' ,in *African Economic History* 4 (1977), pp. 153–71.

White settlers and black peasants: Kenya and Southern Rhodesia (Zimbabwe)

John Lonsdale, 'The Depression and the Second World War in the Transformation of Kenya', in David Killingray and Richard Rathbone (eds)*Africa and the Second World War*, London: Macmillan 1986, pp. 97–142; David Anderson and David Throup, 'The Agrarian Economy of Central

Province, Kenya', in Ian Brown (ed.) op. cit., pp. 8–28; Wolfgang Döpcke, 'Magomo's Maize: State and Peasants during the Depression in Colonial Zimbabwe', in Ian Brown (ed.) op.cit., pp. 29–58. See also Wolfgang Döpcke, *Das koloniale Zimbabwe in der Krise. Eine Wirtschafts- und Sozialgeschichte, 1929–1939*,Münster: Lit 1992.

14 THE POLITICAL CONSEQUENCES OF THE GREAT DEPRESSION: FASCISM IN EUROPE, POPULISM IN LATIN AMERICA AND FREEDOM MOVEMENTS IN THE COLONIES

Fascism in Europe

Wolfgang Schieder,'Das Deutschland Hitlers und das Italien Mussolinis. Zum Problem faschistischer Regimebildung' in Gerhard Schulz (ed.) *Die Große Krise der dreißiger Jahre. Vom Niedergang der Weltwirtschaft zum Zweiten Weltkrieg*, Göttingen: Vandenhoeck 1985, pp. 44–71; Gerhard Schulz, 'Permanente Gleichschaltung des öffentlichen Lebens und Entstehung des nationalsozialistischen Führerstaats in Deutschland', in G. Schulz (ed.) op.cit, pp. 72–100; David Clay Large, *Between Two Fires. Europe's Path in the 1930s*, New York: Norton 1990.

Populism in Latin America

Karl Löwenstein, *Brazil under Vargas,* New York: Macmillan 1942; Arnaldo Cordova, *La politica de masas del cardenismo*, Mexico City: Ediciones Ero 1974; R. H. Dix, *Colombia. The political dimension of change,* New Haven: Yale University Press 1969 (2nd edn).

The colonial freedom movements

D. Rothermund, *Die politische Willensbildung in Indien, 1900–1960*, Wiesbaden: Harrassowitz 1965; D. Rothermund, *Mahatma Gandhi. A political biography*, New Delhi: Manohar 1992; Bernhard Dahm, *A History of Indonesia in the Twentieth Century*, London: Pall Mall Press 1971; T. O. Lloyd, *The British Empire 1558—1983*, Oxford: Oxford University Press 1984; Rudolf von Albertini, *Decolonization. The Administration and Future of the Colonies,1919–1960*, New York: Doubleday 1982 (2nd edn.).

15 FROM DEPRESSION TO WAR: REARMAMENT AND ECONOMIC GROWTH

Armament and inflation: Schacht's clash with Hitler

Andrea Sommariva and Giuseppe Tullio, *German Macro-Economic History 1880–1979*, London: Macmillan 1986. This book contains a translation of the letter written by Schacht to Hitler on 7 January 1939 (p. 247); Hjalmar Schacht, *Abrechnung mit Hitler*, Hamburg: Rowohlt 1948.

Contrasts: Germany and the Western powers

For the data on prices and wages see B.R. Mitchell, *European Historical Statistics 1750–1970*, London: Macmillan 1978. p. 73 ; on Mussolini's war against Abyssinia (Ethiopia) see D.C. Large, op.cit, pp. 138–79; on Hitler's secret memorandum of 1936 see Wilhelm Treue, 'Hitlers Denkschrift zum Vierjahresplan 1936' in *Vierteljahreshefte für Zeitgeschichte* 3 (1955).

A global impact of rearmament?

For the data on Japanese trade with China and the United States see B.R. Mitchell, *International Historical Statistics. Africa and Asia*, London: Macmillan 1982, p. 445.

16 THE AFTERMATH

This last chapter sums up some of the trends discussed in previous ones and requires no references as it is based on the literature cited earlier.

INDEX

Africa 126–35; colonial freedom movements 137–8, 144; colonial rule 126–7, 134–5, 144, 158–9; currencies 127; customary law 126; European trading companies 128–9; import substitution 127; poll tax 129–30

agrarian involution 121, 124, 125

agrarian markets, collapse 14

agriculture 38–47; Argentina 107; Australia 82–3; China 112–13; Egypt 80–1; India 91–2, 155; overproduction 38–9, 82–4; rice 40–2; subsistence 10–11, 98; Turkey 80–1; USA 48, 51, 56, 57–8; wheat 39–40, 82–4

Alejandro, C.F.D. 99

Amery, L. 158

Aranha, O. 103

Argentina 106–8; balance of trade 107; exports 100; Great Britain relationship 107–8; Peronism 141

Asia: colonial freedom movements 137–8; rice production 40–2; Southeast Asia 120–5

Atatürk, K. 74–5

Atlantic Charter 157–8

Australia 82–6; balance of payments crisis 82–3; banks 84–5; devaluation 9, 83, 84–6; 'Grow More Wheat' campaign 82–4; wheat overproduction 82–4

autarky 55, 152

Bagehot, W. 14, 22

Baldwin, S. 33

Bank of England: discount rates 59, 63; gold standard 20–3, 26–9; governor 23; lender of last resort 19–20, 21, 61–2

bank rate 29–30

Bayar, C. 78

'beggar-thy-neighbour' 6–9, 16

Belgian Congo 131–2; export crops 132; forced labour 131

bimetallism 21, 23, 24–6

birth rate 38; Japan 118–19

Brazil 100–3; coffee production 44, 100, 101–2; crisis management 103; Germany trade agreement 101; interventionism 99; populism 141–2; textile industry 101; United States relationship 101–2, 103

Brüning, H. 67–9

Bryan, W.J. 26

Burma: colonial freedom movement 145–6; export economy 122–3; peasant rebellion 122–3; poll tax 122–3; rice exports 122–3; taxation 17; 'Thakins' 146

car industry, USA 49–50

Cardenas, L. 108–9, 143

Ceylon: rubber production 43; tea agreement 95; tea production 43

Chile 105–6; devaluation 9; ore export 106

China 110–15; agriculture 112–13; banks 113–14; cotton production 45; currency 24, 110–11, 113–14; depreciation 111; Japanese penetration 112, 118; Japanese

trade 152–3; Kuomintang 112; land distribution 112; peasants 114; rice production 40; sharecropping 112; silver 24, 110–13, 114; textile industry 112
Churchill, W. 158
cocoa, African production 129–30, 131
coffee: Brazil 44, 100, 101–2; Columbia 44, 105; production 43
colonial freedom movements 144–8
colonialism: economic policy 16; end 156, 157–9; Java 120–1; law 17–18; 'tributes' 20–1
Columbia 103–5; 'Cafeteros' 104; coffee production 44, 105; 'Dance of the Millions' 104; Germany trade agreement 105; interventionism 99, 100; oil 104; populism 142–3
Commonwealth Bank of Australia 83, 84
communism, anti-colonial movements 146–7
conspiracy theories 136
cotton: Egyptian production 45, 79; price collapse 45–6; production 44–6
credit: legal judgements 17–18; web 12–18
Creditanstalt, bankruptcy 61–2
Cuba 99
currency: Africa 127; Bank of England 20; Brazil 103; China 24, 110–11, 113–14; Egypt 78–9; floating 7–8; Germany 139; Great Britain 64; India 87–91; Mexico 108; pegged 7–8; Turkey 77–8; see also bimetallism
Currie, L. 52

Davidson, A.C. 84–5
Dawes Plan 27, 28, 33, 34–6, 66
debt-deflation theory 11, 90–1
deflation: Chile 105–6; France 70–1; gold standard 27, 31; Great Britain 60–1; India 16, 89–91, 93; Japan 41; peasants 11, 46; USA 15; web of credit 13
demographic transition 38
devaluation 7–9; Australia 83, 84–6;

France 70–1; Great Britain 64; Japan 115–18; USA 56–7
Díaz, P. 106, 143
distributional coalitions 67–8

economic disequilibrium theory 3–6
Egypt 74–81; cotton exports 79; cotton production 45; currency 78–9; foreign dependence 74–5; gold export embargo 79–80; grain consumption 80; peasants 80–1; taxation 76
Europe 59–73; decline 162–3; fascism 138–40; political rivalry 36–7; population decline 38; stock market crash effects 59

fascism 137–40
Federal Reserve Board 2; gold standard 15, 22–3; role 14–15; stock market crash 53; structure 51–2
Fisher, I. 11, 51, 53, 90
France 70–1; bimetallic standard 25; colonies 159; Dawes Plan reaction 36; deflation 71; Germany relationship 36, 151–2; gold standard 27, 28; prices 151; Radical Party 71; social democratic party 137; Tripartite Agreement 71; Vietnam 124, 146; wages 151; war debts 32–3
Friedman, M. 53

Gaitan, J.E. 143
Gandhi, M. 145, 157
Geertz, C. 121
Germany 65–70; Brazil trade agreement 101; Columbia trade agreement 105; currency 139; Dawes Plan 27, 28, 34–6; economic crisis 59; fascism 139; foreign exchange controls 62; France relationship 36; gold standard 68–9; inflation 65, 150; political polarisation 67; prices 151; rearmament 149–50, 152–3; reparations 32–6, 65–7; trade relations 68–9; Turkey links 78; wages 151; wheat overproduction 39
Ghana see Gold Coast
Gibson, R. 83
Gilbert, P. 35, 66

gold: 'distress gold' 14, 16, 46, 91;
Egypt 79–80; silver exchange
relation 24–6; sterilisation 15, 22,
28, 54
Gold Coast 129
gold standard 19–31; Bank of
England 20–3, 26–9, 60, 62; Brazil
103; definition 19; Federal Reserve
Board 15, 22–3; France 27, 28;
Germany 68; illusion 19–20; India
88–91; introduction 25–6; Japan
115–16; suspension 15; Sweden 72;
Turkey 77–8; United States 15,
22–3, 26, 27–8, 56–7
government bonds 30
Great Britain 60–5; Argentina
relationship 107–8; banks, crisis
survival 64; capital exports 21;
colonial exploitation 20–1;
colonialism end 157–9; Exchange
Equalisation Account 63; gold
reserves 64; gold standard 20–3,
26–9, 60, 62; India relationship
87–91, 93, 95–7, 157–8; Labour
Party, economic policy 61;
multiple bilateralism 65; neo-
mercantilism 65; prices 151;
protectionism 64–5; wages 60, 151;
war bonds 63–4; war debts 32–6,
63, 66–7, 158

Hamilton, A. 22
Haya de la Torre, V.R. 142
Hindenburg, P. von 69
Hitler, A. 69–70, 139–40; rise to power
149–52
Ho Chi Minh 146
Honduras 99
Hoover, H.C. 55–6
housing construction, USA 50
Hull, C. 102
Hume, D. 19

IJMA see Indian Jute Mills
Association
India 87–97; agricultural prices 155;
British policy consequences 95–7;
colonial freedom movement 95–7,
144–5; colonial rule 144, 157–8;
cotton production 45; council
drafts 88; currency policy 87–91;
deflation 90; depression escape 10;

'distress gold' 16, 91; 'flight from
the rupee' 87, 90; franchise 144–5;
gold exchange standard 25, 88–9;
gold exports 91; import
substitution 93–4; Indian National
Congress 95–6, 144, 145; jute
production 94–5; land revenue 17;
liquidity preference 3–4; peasant
movement 95–6; peasants, debts
90–1; perverse flexibility 90;
purchasing power 93–4; rice 40, 42,
92; rupee value 88–91; Second
World War 157–8; silver currency
24, 25, 87–9; sugar industry 93–4;
sugar production 44; tea
production 43, 95; textile industry
93; wages 10; wheat prices 91–2
Indian Jute Mills Association (IJMA)
94–5
Indonesia see Netherlands Indies
inflation: Germany 65, 150; gold
standard 13; Japan 115; monetary
theory 5; USA 15, 54; web of
credit 13
Inouye 115–16
International Sugar Agreement
(1937) 94
Irigoyen, General 141
Italy: fascism 138; gold standard 28
Ivory Coast 129

Japan 115–19; birth rate 118–19; China
contrast 110; deflation 41; exports
117; foreign trade 152–3; gold
standard 9, 20, 27, 115;
industrialisation 117–18;
population growth 118–19;
rearmament 152–3; rice 39, 40,
41–2; textile industry 112, 117; yen
devaluation 116–17
Java 120–1; agrarian involution 121;
Dutch colonial rule 121; sugar
exports 120–1
Jonge, General de 121
jute, India 94–5

Kennedy, P. 36
Kenya 132–4; hut tax 133; Kikuyu 133;
landowners 132; maize
production 132–3; Mau-Mau
movement 133, 134; poll tax 133;
white settlers 132–3

Keynes, J.M.: Dawes Plan 34;
economic disequilibrium theory
2–6; fascism 139; gold standard 62;
Indian balances 158; mercantilism
65, 107–8
Kreuger, I. 72–3
Kung 113–14

labour market, inelasticities 4–5
land revenue 16–17
Latin America 98–109; import
substitution 98–9; populism 140–4
League of Nations 33
Leguia, President 106
lender of last resort 19–20
liquidity preference 3–4

Macdonald, J.R. 62
McKinley, W. 26
Malaya, rubber production 43
Marhaenism 147
Mau-Mau movement 133, 134
Mecca, Egyptian pilgrims 80
mercantilism 2, 6; see also neo-
mercantilism
Mexico 106, 108–9; balance of trade
108; bimetallic currency 108;
populism 143
Mitsubishi 118
Mitsui corporation 116
monetarism 2
monetary policy: instruments 29–31;
USA 52
monetary theory 3–6; Sweden 71–2
money lenders 10–11, 46–7, 91, 145
Morgan, J.P. 29, 53, 62–3
Mussolini, B. 138

nationalism: fascism 138; India 145,
157
Nehru, J. 96, 138
neo-mercantilism 6–9, 65, 139
Netherlands Indies: colonial freedom
movement 146–7; colonial rule end
159; rubber production 43; sugar
production 44; tea agreement 95;
tea production 43
Newton, I. 25
Niemeyer, O. 85
Nigeria 130
Nissan 118
Norman, M. 23, 26–31, 61–4
Norway, pound link 8

Olaya, President 104
Olson, M. 67
Ottawa Conference (1932) 65

palm kernels 130, 131
Panama 104
Pasha, Z. 74
peanuts 130
peasants: Africa 128–35; Burma
145–6; debts 10–11, 14, 46–7, 90–1,
122; depression effects 10–12;
Egypt 80–1; gold sale 46, 91; India
10, 90–1, 92, 95–6, 144–5; taxation
10–11, 75–6; Turkey 80–1; unrest
11–12, 47, 92, 122, 123–4; Vietnam
123–4
periphery, economic effects 10–12,
46–7, 154–5, 157–9
Peron, J. 141, 142
Peru 105–6; Apristas 142; civil war
106; cotton exports 106; populism
142; reactive state 99–100
Philippines 120, 121; American
colonial rule 121; Manila hemp
121; sugar exports 121
population: decline 38; Japan 118–19
populism: anti-colonial movements
144–6; fascism 138–40; Latin
America 140–4; rise 136–7
Portugal, pound link 8
prices: agriculture 38–47; gold
standard 27; India 91–2; monetary
theory 4–5; USA 54–5; see also
deflation; inflation
Pumarejo, A.L. 142

rearmament, global impact 152–5
Reichsbank 35, 62, 150
reparations 32–7, 66–7
Ricardo, D. 19
rice: Burma 122–3; price collapse
41–2; price protection 92;
production 40–2
Robinson, J. 6–7, 8
Roosevelt, F.D. 154, 156–7; economic
policies 56–8
rubber, production 42–3

Saya San 122–3, 145
scapegoats 136, 137
Schacht, H. 27, 35, 69–70, 139; Hitler
clash 149–50
Schuster, G. 90

4255 075